Dear Zoe,

hope you

**sweet
alternative**

enjoy the book!

Lots of love,

Ariana x x x

ARIANA BUNDY

Photography by Lisa Linder

sweet alternative

In memory of my beautiful grandmother

First published in 2005 by Conran Octopus Ltd
a part of Octopus Publishing Group
2–4 Heron Quays, London E14 4JP
www.conran-octopus.co.uk

Publishing Director Lorraine Dickey
Commissioning Editor Katey Day
Editor Sybella Marlow
Art Director Jonathan Christie
Special Photography Lisa Linder
Food Stylist Ariana Bundy
Stylist Chloe Brown
Production Manager Angela Couchman

British Cataloguing-in-Publication Data.
A catalogue record for this book is available
from the British Library.

ISBN 1 84091 449 1

Printed and bound in China

**All margarine used in these recipes is trans-fat
free and non-hydrogenated, such as Organic
Biona (UK) or Spectrum Spread (US).**

**Recipes have been tested in metric.
Imperial and cup measurements are
approximate equivalents.**

contents

introduction

Dear Reader You are not alone! Up to 75% of the world's population is lactose-intolerant, and those numbers are on the rise. So are allergies and intolerances to soya, the leading dairy substitute in the market today, and gluten found in wheat and other grains. What is the reason for this phenomenon? Could it be that we are more aware of our bodies? Could it also be that our foods and crops are sprayed with chemicals and genetically modified and tampered with, and that our milks are injected with a cocktail of growth hormones and antibiotics? How about preservatives, artificial flavours and additives? Have they weakened our immune systems? Something is definitely happening and we're seeing the changes all around us. We all know someone who is avoiding something in their diet. Articles, menus and new products on supermarket shelves are pointing us towards this shift. Many people are going around with stomach upsets and other gastrointestinal problems, rashes and symptoms of intolerance or allergies, not knowing why they feel the way they do. Many of us have had to make adjustments to our diets, whether small or drastic. It is an uncomfortable feeling not being able to eat and enjoy the foods we used to be able to consume. But as I found out, it can become more uncomfortable consuming those very foods we love.

My Story Sometimes, when people discover a food intolerance or allergy, they gracefully accept the situation and look for other ways to have a normal diet. Often they struggle to keep eating the foods that upset them; feeling unwell, frustrated, even envious of other people who are able to eat anything they like. My situation was more like the latter. 'But I'm a pastry chef, I can't be intolerant to dairy!' All the schooling and rigorous stages and crazy work hours were so that I could enjoy making what I loved eating. My environment and background was in classic French baking, which meant dealing with tons of pure creamery butter and gallons of cream. Now I'm told to steer away from it? I could not imagine going for a day without eating dairy, especially ice cream, my favourite dessert. If I accepted it, that meant drastic changes in my work and in my lifestyle. Doctors also told me to stay away from soya, which is one of the easiest replacements for dairy.

The physical discomfort became too much and finally outweighed the pleasures. No more eating ice cream from the tub or spreading brie on a hot baguette.

Around the same time, my mother and brother were diagnosed with gluten intolerance, so no more fresh croissants and rustic breads for them either. This is what prompted me to start dabbling in unknown territories.

The proof is in the pudding I had to forget almost everything I knew about baking and making desserts. But slowly I began to understand the chemistry that was needed to make alternatives. I adapted myself to a new way of cooking, using new advanced and revamped traditional products but keeping in mind the classic methods and flavour-enhancing ingredients used in French baking. Although I found out that without gluten cakes would never be as fluffy, and that dairy products, especially their milk solids, contribute enormously to the texture and taste of desserts, I pressed on to find the methods that yielded the best results. I realized that with the help of store-bought ingredients such as gluten-free flour, coconut creams and low GI sugars I could come up with desserts that look and taste just like the real thing. Different kinds of syrups, fruit purées, meringues, peels and liqueurs can also add flavour, depth and texture to desserts that might otherwise be flat without the addition of gluten or dairy.

Good News Whatever your reason for switching to a different diet, healthy alternative products and organically grown produce are to hand. Every day there are new products being discovered, evolving and improving all the time, that are of use to diabetics, coeliac and autistic patients, dairy and gluten allergy/sensitive sufferers as well as to religious believers, vegetarians and those who just want to change the way they eat. At natural food shows and events I have met so many passionate individuals creating amazing products that mimic regular foods. Ancient grains and seeds that provide your daily nutrition intake in just one handful. 'Milks' used in desserts that can easily pass for dairy. 'Good fats' that spread and bake beautifully. Outstanding dairy-free chocolates that are also Fair Trade, and vegan gelatines that gel well. This is just the tip of the iceberg for you and me!

In a Nutshell By being a smart cookie, you too can find out how to overcome allergies and intolerances and learn how to bake in a new way. Being dairy-intolerant was, in a funny way, one of the best things that could have happened to me. It opened my eyes to a different world of healthy alternative ingredients and new ways of eating and thinking.

Whatever your reason for cutting out certain foods, this book allows you to have your cake and eat it! You'll not only feed your cravings but also make your cooking experience so enjoyable that you'll never look at another cream bun with regret again.

Ariana

arm yourself

First you'll want to find out what products are available to replace the ones you can no longer eat. You'll be amazed, as I was, to see what's being produced to mimic the old classics. Try to buy organic whenever you can, as it tastes better and is healthier for your body and for the environment.

The ingredients in this book and the products below are 100% natural with no artificial colours, flavours or preservatives.

GET STARTED!

You don't need to arm yourself with many things to be able to make the recipes in this book. To make your life easier, here is a breakdown and glossary of some of the ingredients that are available. One ingredient from each catagory can get you started.

FLOURS

- **Gluten-free flours** you can buy pre-mixed (see Top Sites and Addresses page 184). I like to add 35 g/1¼ oz/⅓ cup of sweet rice flour (mochiko) to every 2 cups of store-bought gluten-free mix.
- You can also **mix your own**, as follows: Mix 225 g/8 oz/2 cups rice flour with 70 g/2½ oz/⅔ cup sweet rice flour, 70 g/2½ oz/⅔ cup potato starch flour (not to be confused with potato flour), and 35 g/1¼ oz/⅓ tapioca flour. Store in the refrigerator or freezer in an airtight container and bring to room temperature before using.

'MILKS'

These are great to bake with, and also create authetic creams and custards. They are also very low in fat and some are virtually fat-free. Look for calcium-enriched ones to replace needed calcium.
- **Liquid** includes almond, rice, quinoa and hazelnut milks. Coconut milk has about 17% fat and comes in cans or cartons. Make sure you buy

the ones that have no emulsifiers or additives and are just labelled 'coconut and water'. Coconut cream (24% fat or more) also comes in cans or cartons and is similar to double (heavy) cream. Not to be confused with creamed coconut, which comes in a hard block.
- **Powders** such as Ecomilk, Vance's DariFree, coconut milk powder, Better Than Milk rice powder and Nutquick all do the trick. Powdered milks have the added bonus that you can control the final thickness of the milk according to the amount of water you add.

FATS

- **Margarine** make sure you use trans-fat-free margarine. Non-hydrogenated margarine such as Organic Biona (UK) or Spectrum Spread (US) contains coconut butter and palm oil, although Spectrum Spread contains soy protein.
- **Ghee**, although pure dairy, this contains no milk solids because it's 98% fat and 2% water. It's wonderful to bake with and gives a buttery flavour to things without the milk solids. If you are allergic or intolerant to dairy products, please check with your doctor before using ghee.
- **Coconut** butter or oil has a hard white texture at room temperature, melts easily and has a lovely clean taste. It has come back into the spotlight as having amazing health benefits, because it's full of essential amino acids and vitamins. Look for non-virgin, expeller-pressed, naturally refined, non-hydrogenated coconut butter which has a neutral taste and no trans-fatty acids.
- **Oils** naturally refined high-oleic sunflower and safflower oils, and olive oils are wonderful to bake with. Other oils, such as hemp, flaxseed (linseed), hazelnut and walnut, are best used in very small quantities to flavour or fortify the final product.

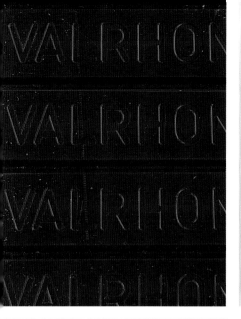

SUGARS

- **Granular sugar** comes in light, brown, demerara and muscovado types. Most recipes in this book use unrefined raw caster sugar.
- **Icing (confectioners') sugar** golden icing sugar is available, but you can also make it at home by simply grinding caster (superfine) sugar in a pestle and mortar or a clean coffee grinder.
- **Agave nectar** this Mexican wonder sometimes goes by the name of agave syrup. In fact, it looks like thick sugar syrup and is 25% sweeter than sugar. Use light agave, not the dark molasses kind.
- **Rice syrup** sweet and mellow. Make sure it's barley-free.
- **Maple syrup** comes as the usual syrup and also in granulated form.
- **Raw honey** untreated, unpasteurized natural honey is best. Also comes in granulated form.

FLAVOURS

- **Nuts and seeds**
These come as flours (defatted) and ground, to be used as milk or folded into cake mixtures. They also come as whole nuts, hulled, nibs, slivers, flakes, butters and milks. They range from hazelnuts, almonds, walnuts and macadamias to pumpkin seeds, sesame and hulled hemp seeds. Unsweetened coconut powder is a fabulous way to add depth to many of your desserts. Buy it shredded, and pulse it in a food processor if fine powder is called for.
- **Chocolate** Buy the best dark chocolate you can, ideally 70% cocoa solids (see Top Sites page 184). Organic chocolate with a Fair Trade logo is the best! Alternatively, carob powder or drops are a good substitute for chocolate.
- **Egg replacer** Ener-G brands have a product called Egg Replacer. Although it does not really replace eggs in recipes that call for more than 1 egg, it does give extra leavening to baked goods.
- **Flax meal/ground flax seeds** (linseeds) are a good substitute for eggs. Simply mix 50 g/2 oz/ ½ cup flax meal/ground flax seeds (linseeds) with 350 ml/12 fl oz/1½ cup boiling water and use in recipes that can be replaced by it. Its usually not suitable for recipes that call for 2 eggs or more.

GELATINES

Many choices, but some work better in certain recipes than others.

- **Traditional** powder and leaves made from beef or pork. 1 gelatine leaf = 1 teaspoon powder, and 1 tablespoon powder = 4 leaves. Another option is Aquagel, which is made from fish.
- **Vegan** Agar agar comes in block, flake or fine powder form. 'Agars' vary in strength and need to be cooked for a few minutes in order to set. 1 teaspoon agar powder = 1 tablespoon agar flakes. The Esmel brand is made from locust bean and carrageen gum.

BAKING CATALYSTS

- **Xanthan gum** a natural, glue-like powder that acts like the gluten found in wheat. You can use guar gum in exactly the same way. It is also used as a binder in ice creams and a thickener in sauces.
- **Salep** the root of an orchid variety, this is sold in most Middle Eastern shops and comes in rock-like granules or powder form. Although commonly used in summer drinks and ice creams, I've found it to be a very good substitute for xanthan gum.
- **Baking powder and bicarbonate of soda (baking soda)** make sure you buy baking powder and bicarbonate of soda that's gluten-free as well as aluminium-free.

FOOD COLOURING AND DECORATIONS

- These come as **pastes** and **powders** and also as sugar **crystals** and **beads.** There are some really fascinating products using natural colouring ingredients such as spinach, beetroot, blueberries and turmeric.
- **Natural gold and silver leaves** can instantly glamorize your baking and are safe to eat. See Top Sites on page 184 for purchasing information.

What's Hot

Below is a safe list of all gluten- dairy- and soy-free foods currently available or up and coming in healthfood stores near you. See Top Sites and Addresses (page 184) for details on where to locate these ingredients.

FLOURS

- adzuki flour
- amaranth: flour, grain, puffs
- buckwheat: flour, flakes, groats
- sweet rice flour (sticky rice, glutinous rice or Mochiko)
- corn: yellow or blue meal, polenta, starch, grits
- defatted coconut flour
- garbanzo or chickpea flour
- garfava (bean flour)
- meals or powders of almond, hazelnut, cashew nut, chestnut
- millet: flour, grains, flakes
- montina flour
- Old Indian Flour Mixes (mix of gram dahls)
- potato flour
- potato starch flour
- quinoa: flour, seeds, flakes, puffs
- rice flakes (poha), puffs
- rice flour: white, brown
- sorghum
- tapioca flour
- teff
- yam

MILKS

- almond milk
- coconut milk and cream
- Nutriz M rice protein powder
- quinoa milk
- potato milk (Vance's DariFree)
- rice milk
- sesame milk
- tiger nut milk

FATS

- coconut butter (extra-virgin or regular)
- extra-virgin olive oil
- flax oil and meal
- ghee
- grapeseed oil
- hemp oil
- high-oleic oils
- margarine, trans-fat free brands
- red palm oil
- rice bran oil

SUGARS

- agave: nectar (light and dark) and granulated
- coconut syrup
- FOS (Fructo Oligo Saccharide)
- honey: liquid and granulated
- Luo Han Guo (glycemic natural sweetener)
- maple: granulated and syrup
- date: granulated and syrup
- rapadurra
- rice syrup
- sorghum molasses
- stevia (a noncaloric herb used as a sweetener)
- tapioca syrup
- unrefined caster, muscovado, brown, Demerara, powdered
- yakon potato/yacon potato (a root vegetable sweetener in syrup form safe for diabetics)

FLAVOURS

- allspice
- candied oranges
- carob powder and chips
- citrus zest
- dark chocolate: chips and blocks
- dried unsulphurized fruits, raisins, mango, apricots, dates, coconut powder or flakes
- gluten-free vanilla extract
- gluten-free un-alkalized cocoa powder
- green tea powder and leaf
- liqueurs: kirsch, Cointreau, Grand Marnier
- orange blossom water
- rose water
- saffron powder or threads
- white chocolate by Oppenheimer (contains soy lecithin)

STORE-BOUGHT

- adzuki beans or paste
- agar agar: powder. flakes, brick and new 'leaves'
- arrowroot or Kuzu
- baby fruit purees (unsweetened)
- baking powder and bicarbonate of soda/baking soda (gluten-free and aluminium-free)
- bee pollen
- coloured sugar crystals
- egg replacer
- Fleurs de Sels salt or Japanese Okinawan Shio salt
- food colourings
- gelatine leaves or powder
- goji berries
- gold and silver leaf
- ice cream cones (gluten-free)
- Kaki Mochi (Japanese rice crackers)
- pistachio paste
- pre-made nut butters
- rice bran
- rice paper
- rice protein powder
- salep powder (orchid root)
- sweetened chestnut: candied, puree (not paste)
- spirulina powder
- tapioca pearls
- xanthan gum

1

cookie jar

It's OK to get caught with your hand in this jar – **decadent** chocolate cookies, moist coconut morsels, French macarons, high-protein bars, gooey brownies, almond chews and more. We all have **fond memories** of cookies because they were probably one of the first things we were allowed to bake as children. So for those who can no longer eat gluten, the world can turn a little upside down. Stick to these **simple steps** for perfect cookies: use a silicon liner such as Exopat or a non-stick baking tray. Always use eggs and margarine at **room temperature**. It's better to have your cookies under- rather than over-baked. **Chill** the dough for at least two hours before using. Roll, pre-cut and **freeze** the dough before storing in airtight containers. Now cookies are back on the menu. Make them for your **loved** ones and watch their faces light up! Just follow these simple gluten-free recipes to bake cookies that taste just like your **childhood favourites**.

Protein-packed Peanut Butter Cookies

These dense, nutty cookies have almost the same texture as a sports bar but taste fresher. They fuel and fill you up for a long time, as they are packed with nuts and quinoa. Instead of peanut butter you can use other nut butters such as cashew and almond.

MAKES 36

60 g/2 oz/½ cup lightly roasted quinoa flakes

160 g/5 oz/1¼ cups gluten-free flour

½ teaspoon baking powder

⅓ teaspoon xanthan gum

80 g/3 oz/⅓ cup margarine or ghee or coconut butter

200 g/7 oz/½ cup demerara sugar

200 g/7 oz/1 cup light brown sugar

1 organic egg + 1 organic egg white

1 teaspoon vanilla extract

60 ml/4 tablespoons/¼ cup rice milk, or any non-dairy milk substitute

180 g/6 oz/½ cup peanut butter

Preheat the oven to 180°C/350°F/gas mark 4. Line a baking tray with a silicon liner, or get a non-stick baking tray ready.

Dry-toast your quinoa in a hot pan for 1–2 minutes. Let it cool. Sift the flour, baking powder and xanthan gum into a bowl. Stir in the quinoa until well blended, and set aside.

Cream the margarine or ghee and the sugars until fluffy. Beat in the whole egg, egg white and vanilla extract until creamy, then add the peanut butter and rice milk. Add the quinoa mixture and blend well. Drop walnut-sized spoonfuls on to the prepared baking tray 5 cm/2 inches apart, flatten the tops a little with the back of a fork, and bake in the preheated oven for about 8–10 minutes. The cookies will be golden brown and will harden as they cool, so don't be tempted to bake them for longer. They taste better when they are still soft in the middle.

Leave the cookies to cool on the baking tray before transferring to a wire rack to cool completely. These cookies are best eaten fresh, or frozen immediately.

Chocolate Chilli Cookies

I love watching people eat these cookies. First they take a bite, expecting the familiar taste of a simple chocolate cookie. Then their face changes: they stop chewing, frown, and stare at the cookie with a startled expression as if someone has been playing a trick on them. Then, just when you think they're going to put it down, they take another bite and pick up another one! The heat of the chilli goes amazingly well with the chocolate, which is not surprising because the ancient Aztecs and Mayans used to mix 'xocoatl' (Mayan word for chocolate) with chillies before the Spaniards took it to Europe and added sugar to it instead.

MAKES 36

260 g/9 oz/2 cups gluten-free flour

1 teaspoon bicarbonate of soda (baking soda)

¼ teaspoon cayenne pepper or ancho chilli powder

45 g/1½ oz/⅓ cup cocoa powder

½ teaspoon xanthan gum

½ teaspoon ground cinnamon

dash of nutmeg

pinch of sea salt

225 g/8 oz/1 cup margarine or ghee or coconut butter, at room temperature

175 g/6 oz/1 cup muscovado or palm sugar or rapadura sugar

1 organic egg

2 teaspoons vanilla extract

200 g/7 oz/1⅔ cups roughly chopped dark (bittersweet) chocolate or chocolate chips

Sift together the flour, bicarbonate of soda, cayenne or chilli, cocoa powder, xanthan gum, cinnamon, nutmeg and salt, and set aside.

Cream the margarine or ghee until pale, then add the sugar and whisk until creamy. Blend together the egg and vanilla extract and whisk into the mixture. With a wooden spoon, fold in first the dry mixture, then the chocolate chips. Put the mixture into the refrigerator to firm up before baking.

Meanwhile, preheat the oven to 180°C/350°F/gas mark 4. Line a baking tray with a silicon liner, or get a non-stick baking tray ready.

Spoon out rounded tablespoons of the dough on to the prepared baking tray 6 cm/2½ inches apart and bake in the preheated oven for 10 minutes.

Leave the cookies to cool on the baking tray before transferring to a wire rack to cool completely. These cookies are best eaten fresh, or frozen immediately.

Chocolate Chip Cookies with Roasted Walnuts

I bake these delicious no-frills cookies for my brother, who is gluten-intolerant. He recently stopped eating wheat and products containing gluten, since his body cannot tolerate pasta, bread, cookies, muffins and so on. To cope with his withdrawal symptoms I created this recipe, reminiscent of the Nestlé Toll House cookies we used to make as kids during those long summer afternoons in New England, when we would ransack the kitchen. Gluten is what gives baked goods lightness and tenderness; otherwise you end up with super dry and crumbly end results. You can add xanthan gum, a naturally derived ingredient similar to glue now widely used in the American gluten-free industry. In this recipe I tried salep, the powdered root of a wild orchid variety, generally used in certain summer drinks or Persian ice cream but never in baked goods. I must say that my experiment yielded very similar results! Salep powder is available in all Middle Eastern shops.

MAKES 36

225 g/8 oz/1 cup coconut butter at room temperature, or slightly cold ghee or margarine

130 g/4½ oz/¾ cup brown sugar

45 g/1½ oz/⅓ cup dark Muscovado sugar

115 g/4 oz/½ cup unrefined golden caster (superfine) sugar

2 small organic eggs, beaten with 2 teaspoons vanilla extract

3 tablespoons unsweetened apple purée

260 g/9 oz/2 cups gluten-free flour

45 g/1½ oz/⅓ cup sweet rice flour (mochiko)

1 teaspoon bicarbonate of soda (baking soda)

pinch of sea salt

½ teaspoon xanthan gum, or ½ teaspoon salep powder

450 g/1 lb dark (bittersweet) chocolate, minimum 66% cocoa solids (for example, Valrhona's Caraïbe or Manjari, or other good-quality chocolate), roughly chopped

100 g/2½ oz/⅔ cup roasted walnuts, roughly chopped

Preheat the oven to 180°C/350°F/gas mark 4. Prepare a baking tray or line a tray with a silicon liner.

In a large bowl, cream the coconut butter with the sugars until light and fluffy. Add the egg and vanilla extract mixture, in stages so it doesn't curdle. If it does, simply beat hard for a few seconds. Make sure to occasionally scrape the sides as you do this, to ensure even blending. Now add the apple purée.

Sift the flour, bicarbonate of soda, salt and xanthan gum or salep, and gently mix in. Fold in the chocolate and walnuts. Place tablespoons of the mixture 6 cm/2½ inches apart on the prepared baking tray, flatten them with the back of a fork, and bake in the preheated oven for about 12–15 minutes or until golden. A good method to ensure even-sized cookies is to use a small ice cream scoop or even a melon baller for mini versions. Leave the cookies to cool on the baking tray before transferring to a wire rack to cool completely. Store in an aitight container for up to three days.

Variations

Substitute the dark chocolate with white chocolate or carob chips. You can also add dried sour cherries or orange peel to the batter. Roasted quinoa flakes can replace ½ gluten-free flour for added crunch.

Mock Oatmeal Cookies

Flakes made from gluten-free grains are so similar to oatmeal that you won't be able to tell the difference. I love eating these cookies with a glass of cold almond milk.

MAKES 36

85 g/3 oz/¾ cup sorghum flour

40 g/1½ oz/⅓ cup sweet rice flour or tapioca flour

½ teaspoon xanthan gum

1½ teaspoons bicarbonate of soda (baking soda)

1 teaspoon cinnamon

85 g/3 oz/¾ cup poha, quinoa or buckwheat flakes

175 ml/6 fl oz/½ cup honey or agave nectar, or 75 ml/3 fl oz/¼ cup maple syrup

115 g/4 oz/½ cup margarine or ghee or coconut butter

65 g/2½ oz/⅓ cup unrefined light brown sugar

115 g/4 oz/½ cup Cashew Butter (page 150) or any other store-bought nut butter

1 teaspoon vanilla extract

pinch of sea salt

Preheat the oven to 170°C/325°F/gas mark 3. Line a baking tray with a silicon liner, or get a non-stick baking tray ready. Sift the flours, xanthan gum, bicarbonate of soda, cinnamon and salt and set aside.

Mix the poha, quinoa or buckwheat flakes with the honey or agave nectar and set aside. Meanwhile, cream the margarine with the sugar until creamy, add the cashew butter and the vanilla extract, and mix for a few seconds more. Add the flake mixture to the creamed mixture, then stir in the sifted flour mixture. Place tablespoons of dough on the prepared tray and bake in the preheated oven for about 10–12 minutes. The cookies may appear soft but will harden as they cool.

Leave the cookies to cool on the baking tray before transferring to a wire rack to cool completely. These cookies are best eaten fresh. Store in an airtight container for up to three days.

Coconut Rochers ♡

Meaning 'rocks' in French, these easy-to-make coconut morsels look like little mountains and have no added fat. They're caramelized and slightly crunchy on the outside, and super-moist and fluffy on the inside. They freeze exceptionally well as a dough or cooked.

MAKES 30–35 MINI ROCHERS

300 g/10 oz/3½ cups unsweetened desiccated coconut

250 g/9 oz/1 cup golden caster (superfine) sugar

115 g/4 oz/approx 4 organic egg whites

3 tablespoons unsweetened apple purée

Preheat your oven to 200°/400F/gas mark 6. Line a baking tray with a silicon liner, or get a non-stick baking tray ready.

In a large bowl mix the coconut and sugar until well blended. Add the egg whites and apple purée and mix evenly. In a microwave, or a bain-marie, heat the mixture for 3 minutes, stirring with a wooden spoon after each minute. Carefully insert your finger or a thermometer into the middle of the coconut mixture, and if it's hot to the touch or 50°C/120°F, it's ready. Let it cool to room temperature. What you are doing is par-cooking the egg whites so that even though they are quickly 'flashed' in the very hot oven, they're cooked, stay moist on the inside and become golden on the outside.

Use a piping bag without a nozzle, a mini scoop, or a tablespoon to place half-walnut-sized dollops of the mixture on the baking tray. With damp fingers, shape them into little mountains or uneven pyramids. Cook in the preheated oven for around 8–10 minutes or until lightly golden, turning the tray once halfway through the cooking time.

Remove the rochers from the baking tray and place on to a wire rack to cool. Store in an airtight container for up to five days.

Variations

You can add chocolate chips to the cooled mixture or, for a delicious molten centre, place a teaspoon of refrigerated Dark Chocolate Ganache (page 144) in the centre of the dough before shaping.

For a beautiful finish, dip the tip of each cooked and cooled coconut rocher in melted chocolate. The choices are endless… The mixture freezes beautifully for up to a month.

'Raw' Honey Florentines

These florentines really pass the taste test, tasting absolutely the same as the original recipe which uses tons of butter and cream! You'll find these crunchy clusters and their creamy honey sweetness, irresistible. If you prefer, you can omit the honey and replace it with an equal amount of rice syrup instead. For more elaborate florentines, pour the hot mixture into a pre-cooked pastry case and cut into mini squares with a sharp heavy knife, to serve.

MAKES 24 MEDIUM OR 48 SMALL FLORENTINES

4 tablespoons full-fat coconut milk

85 g/3 oz raw unfiltered honey

2 tablespoons rice syrup

85 g/3 oz/$\frac{1}{3}$ cup unrefined golden caster (superfine) sugar

1 teaspoon vanilla extract

60 g/2 oz/$\frac{1}{4}$ cup margarine or ghee or coconut butter

45 g/$\frac{1}{2}$ oz/$\frac{1}{4}$ cup raisins

60 g/2 oz/$\frac{1}{3}$ cup candied orange peel

150 g/5 oz/$\frac{1}{4}$ cup lightly toasted almond flakes

Line a baking tray with a silicon liner. Alternatively, rub a little oil over a non-stick baking tray or marble countertop.

In a large pan over a medium heat, boil the coconut milk, honey, rice syrup, sugar, vanilla extract, and margarine or ghee or coconut butter until light amber. This will take about 10–15 minutes. Stir the liquid from time to time and make sure you watch the last few minutes of cooking, as the mixture can darken rather quickly. Take the pan off the heat and add the remaining ingredients in one go. Quickly mix with a wooden spoon. Make sure you use toasted nuts so that the end result is crunchy rather than too chewy. With the help of two spoons, place walnut-sized dollops on the tray and let them cool.

Once cold, you can spread the bottom of the florentines with melted chocolate and leave them to harden. Store in an airtight container for up to one week.

Variations

Try adding toasted coconut flakes and sun-dried mangoes for a fruitier, more tropical flavour.

French Macarons

These are totally different to American macaroons. They are light, slightly chewy and airy on the inside, while remaining delicately crisp on the outside. In some Parisian pastry stores, they're proudly stacked on top of each other in the shape of the Eiffel Tower, in a display of the store's craftsmanship. They come in different pastel colours, each with its own distinct flavour and buttercream or jam filling. Macarons are also traditionally gluten-free! They were first made in monasteries in the 8th Century. By the 17th Century they were manufactured by the Carmelites who believed that 'almonds were good for girls who do not eat meat'. I acquired the following recipe while working in patissèrie at Le Notre, a restaurant in Paris, where they're noted for their outstanding macarons.

MAKES 60

200 g/7 oz/1¾ cups unrefined golden icing (confectioners') sugar

150 g/5 oz/1¼ cups ground almonds

45 g/1½ oz/⅓ cup caster (superfine) sugar

1 vanilla pod

4 organic egg whites

½ x recipe Vanilla Buttercream (page 155)

Preheat the oven to 200°C/400°F/gas mark 6. Line two baking trays with a silicon liner, or get non-stick baking trays ready.

In a large bowl, mix together the icing sugar ground almonds. (You can now buy golden icing sugar in health food stores, or make your own by blending brown sugar in your coffee grinder. Use white icing sugar if brown is not available.)

Split open the vanilla pod along its length. Using the tip of your knife, scrape out the seeds and add them to the almond and sugar mix.

In a dry clean bowl, whisk the egg whites with a pinch of caster sugar until foamy. This is the point to add any colouring or flavours, such as chocolate or raspberry (see variations page 30). Whisk the egg whites to soft peaks, adding the remaining caster sugar in stages. This will give a lovely shiny meringue.

Pour the almond and sugar mixture on to the meringue in one go and quickly and gently fold in with a large spatula. Scoop the mixture into a pastry bag fitted with a simple nozzle, and pipe out small 2.5 cm/1 inch buttons evenly all over the baking trays. Gently tap the trays once to even them out a bit, but not more or it will knock the air out of the macarons. Leave them to stand for 15–20 minutes, then bake in the preheated oven for about 8–10 minutes or until lightly golden in colour.

Remove from the oven, gently lift one corner of the parchment paper and pour a cup of water on to the hot tray. This will create a little steam, which will facilitate the removal of the sticky macarons. (You can bypass this step if you have a silicon liner!) Remove the macarons immediately to a wire rack and cool completely. Store in an airtight container for up to five days.

Once the macarons are cool, pair off the ones closest in size and pipe a hazelnut-sized knob of vanilla buttercream on to one half. Gently twist and press the two macarons together. They freeze for up to three weeks so amazingly well that you'll want to remove everything in your freezer to make room for them.

Rainbow of Macarons

Macarons, as you know, have been popular for years. But now they have become almost a cult. Designers such as Christian Lacroix and Sonya Rykiel are designing macarons and other sweets for famous Paris pastry houses. The situation is so surreal that I had to call one of the shops in Paris to check whether it was my imagination, or whether I truly did see 'Lacroix' signed on one of the boxes! Chefs like Pierre Hermé are coming up with very interesting flavour combinations as well, such as olive oil and vanilla, passion fruit and chocolate, macha green tea and chestnut, and even toasted sesame.

Using the previous macarons recipe as a base, you can create all sorts of different flavours.

Chocolate

Reduce the quantity of icing sugar and ground almonds by 30 g/1 oz/¼ cup and replace with an equal amount of cocoa powder. Fill the macarons with a noisette of Dark Chocolate Ganache (page 144).

Raspberry

Add a few drops of beetroot colouring to the finished meringue mixture and 3 tablespoons of raspberry purée to the buttercream. You can also fill the macarons with store-bought raspberry jam instead of buttercream.

Coffee

Add ¼ teaspoon of coffee extract to both the meringue mixture and the buttercream. You can also fill the macarons with Dark Chocolate Ganache (page 144).

Pistachio and Orange-blossom

Reduce the quantity of ground almonds by 60 g/2 oz/½ cup and add the same amount of ground pistachios. Add a few drops of spinach food colouring and mix. Add 1 rounded tablespoon of ground pistachios or 2 teaspoons of pistachio paste and 1 teaspoon of orange-blossom water to the buttercream before filling the macarons.

Macha Green Tea and Chestnut Cream

Add 1 teaspoon of macha green tea powder to the almond and sugar mixture before adding the egg whites. For the filling, mix the vanilla buttercream with the same amount of chestnut purée, stir in 1–2 drops of lemon extract and fill the macarons with the mixture.

Lemon Bars

These are really quick to make, like mini lemon tarts but chunkier. You can use any lemon cream you have left over for this recipe. 'Buttery' and tart, these creamy bars are absurdly delicious. You can replace the lemons in the lemon cream recipe with blood oranges, lime or even passion fruit for a whole different take.

MAKES 12–16 BARS

260 g/9 oz/2 cups gluten-free flour

pinch of sea salt

1 teaspoon vanilla sugar

115 g/4 oz/½ cup unrefined golden icing (confectioners') sugar

½ teaspoon xanthan gum

175 g/6 oz/¾ cup cold margarine, ghee or coconut butter, cubed

1 x recipe Lucious Lemon Cream (page 152)

Preheat the oven to 180°C/350°F/gas mark 4. Lightly grease a 20 cm/8 inch square cake tin and set aside.

Mix the flour, sea salt, vanilla sugar, sugar and xanthan gum. Place in a bowl along with the margarine, ghee or coconut butter. Crumble the mixture, using your fingers or a cutter, until it looks like coarse breadcrumbs. You can also do this in a food processor.

Spread the mixture in the prepared tin, pushing it down into the corners.

Bake in the preheated oven for about 15 minutes until pale gold. Remove from the oven, pour the lemon cream on top, and bake for another 20 minutes. Let the cake cool completely before cutting it into squares. If you like, you can sprinkle the top with some icing (confectioners') sugar.

Quinoa Crispy Treats

A smarter version of a Rice Krispie treat, one that doesn't have the sugar shock of the marshmallows and corn syrup. They're made with peanut butter, but almond, cashew or hemp butter can easily be substituted measure for measure. You can substitute all kinds of things for the sweet and tangy dried apricots: candied oranges, dried apple chips, dried mangoes, chopped dates, raisins, sesame seeds, slivered almonds – basically anything you want or have to hand. Quinoa contains a lot of protein and magnesium, and rice syrup has a sweet and mellow taste that doesn't overpower the sweetness of the dried fruits.

MAKES 9 LARGE OR 12 SMALL SQUARES

115 g/4 oz/½ cup natural peanut, almond, cashew or hemp butter

½ teaspoon vanilla extract

115 ml/4 fl oz/½ cup rice syrup

200 g/7 oz/3½ cups puffed quinoa or gluten-free rice puffs

85 g/3 oz/½ cup dried unsulphured dried apricots, finely chopped

Lightly grease a 20 cm/8 inch square cake tin and set aside.

Place the nut butter, vanilla extract and rice syrup in a bain-marie (a bowl set in a pan of simmering water) or a microwave and heat till hot and boiling. Remove from the heat and quickly stir in the puffed quinoa or rice puffs and the chopped apricots.

Pour into the prepared tin and push down with your fingers to fill up the edges and smooth out the top. Grease your fingers as you do this so that the mixture doesn't stick. It's really that easy.

Let it cool before cutting out crispy squares.

Flower Power

These shortbread cookies are shaped like flowers, and because they are made with pure chickpea flour they are packed with protein. They contain no eggs and are melt-in the-mouth tender and soft. This is a traditional Persian recipe that's served at special ceremonies such as weddings and New Year. They're incredibly easy to prepare and last for months stored in the freezer.

MAKES 35–40

450 g/1 lb/4 cups fine roasted chickpea flour

350 g/12 oz/1½ cups unrefined golden caster (superfine) sugar

2½ teaspoons vanilla sugar

115 g/4 oz/½ cup coconut butter or ghee

3 tablespoons slivered pistachio nuts, for decoration

If you can't find roasted chickpea flour, simply place the unroasted flour on a baking tray and bake in a 180°C/350°F/gas mark 4 oven for about 12–15 minutes or until golden.

The next step can be done either by hand or with a KitchenAid (or other food mixer) fitted with a paddle. Place the caster sugar, vanilla sugar and coconut butter or ghee in the mixing bowl and mix for about 2–3 minutes (or 5 minutes by hand) until pale and creamy. Add the chickpea flour and mix for a further 3 minutes or until a dough forms. Don't be tempted to add any liquid – a dough will form eventually. Place the dough on a floured board and knead for another minute or so until it is no longer sticky. Line a baking tray with baking parchment and push and flatten the dough so that it is about 2.5cm/1 inch thick. Place in the refrigerator for at least 1 hour.

Meanwhile, preheat the oven to 150°C/300°F/gas mark 2. Line a baking tray with a silicon liner, or get a non-stick baking tray ready. Take the dough out of the refrigerator and cut out clover-leaves or flowers. Place them on the prepared baking tray – they won't rise or spread much, so leave just 1–2 cm/an inch or so between them. Bake them in the preheated oven for about 25–30 minutes.

Don't allow the cookies to colour – check them underneath, and if they're golden and slightly pinkish, they're done. Take them out of the oven and push one pistachio sliver into the middle of each cookie. Leave to cool completely before removing them from the tray or they will crumble. They keep for about one month in the refrigerator or three months in the freezer.

Fresh Ginger Spice Cookies

This is for all those ginger-lovers out there. I recently met someone at a food show who owns his own ginger plantation on the island of Fiji. He produces the loveliest ginger products, ranging from candied ginger to stem ginger and fresh juice. He spends a few months a year in California and the rest at home in paradise!

This cookie is sweetened with sorghum molasses. It tastes like regular molasses but isn't a by-product of cane sugar. In fact, you can replace it in any recipe that calls for molasses. See Top Sites and Addresses (page 184) to hunt this delicious liquid down.

MAKES 36

300 g/10 oz/2⅓ cups gluten-free flour

2 teaspoons ground ginger

2 teaspoons bicarbonate of soda (baking soda)

1 teaspoon xanthan gum

pinch of sea salt

200 g/8 oz/1 cup dark brown sugar

175 g/6 oz/¾ cup margarine or ghee or coconut oil, at room temperature

1 large organic egg

1½ tablespoons finely chopped fresh root ginger

85 g/3 oz/½ cup stem ginger, finely chopped

115 ml/4 fl oz/⅓ cup sorghum molasses

1 teaspoon vanilla extract

Sift the flour, ground ginger, bicarbonate of soda and xanthan gum together with the pinch of sea salt and set aside.

In a KitchenAid (or other food mixer) fitted with a paddle attachment or using an hand-held electric whisk, cream the sugar with the ghee, margarine or coconut oil until creamy. Add the egg and beat until incorporated. Add the fresh and stem ginger, sorghum molasses, vanilla extract and mix. With the machine running on low, add the dry mixture until there is no visible trace of flour left.

Wrap the dough and chill for several hours.

Preheat the oven to 170°C/325°F/gas mark 3. Line a baking tray with a silicon liner, or get a non-stick baking sheet ready. Take the dough out of the refrigerator, pinch off tablespoonfuls and roll them into balls.

You can either place the balls on the prepared tray as they are, or roll them in some golden granulated sugar first. The latter method will give a crunchier cookie. Leave a 5–8 cm/2–3 inch space between the cookies and bake in the preheated oven for about 12–15 minutes. The cookies will harden as they cool. Wait till they are at room temperature before taking them off the tray. These cookies are best stored in an airtight container in the freezer for up to two days.

Saffron and Pistachio Bars ♡

This is just one example of what you can make in a bar form. Try tahini butter, made with sesame seeds, instead of cashew or almond butter. For different flavours, add shredded coconut with chopped dried mangoes or papayas, and macadamias instead of pistachios. The dough is very forgiving, just pat it down evenly and you have nothing to worry about.

MAKES 16-18 SQUARES

2–3 saffron threads or the tip of a sharp knife's worth of saffron powder

juice and zest of ½ lemon, finely chopped

½ teaspoon rose water

225 g/8 oz/1 cup raw Cashew or Almond Butter (page 150)

60 g/2 oz/½ cup raw pistachios, very finely chopped

60 g/2 oz/½ cup raw almonds, very finely chopped

70 g/2½ oz/½ cup soft dried dates, pitted and very finely chopped or puréed

225 g/8 oz/¼ cup agave nectar

dash of sea salt

1 x recipe Cashew Nut Glaze (page 151)

Start by grinding the saffron with the lemon zest and juice in a pestle and mortar, for a minute or so. This releases the aromas of the zest and saffron. Add the rose water and sea salt and stir a little. Put all the rest of the ingredients into a bowl, add the saffron mixture, and knead with your hands for about 2 minutes. This can be done in a KitchenAid (or other food mixer) fitted with a paddle attachment, if you don't want saffron-stained fingers. Mix until smooth.

Line a 20 cm/8 inch square cake tin with some clingfilm. Put in the dough mixture and push it down into the tin. If using the Cashew Nut Glaze, spread evenly on top. Cover it with another layer of clingfilm making sure it doesn't touch the top of the mixture and put it into the refrigerator for about 4 hours. Remove from the tin, take off the clingfilm and cut into squares or diamonds. You can decorate with more pistachios if you like.

Funky Popcorn Clusters

I love the combination of sweet and salty snacks, like honey and mustard pretzels or fleurs de sel (sea salt) caramel, and this recipe follows the same pattern – though it takes it to a whole new level with some very unusual ingredients. This recipe reminds me of good old-fashioned American Cracker Jacks, but it's more grown-up and much better for you because it uses rice syrup, not high-glycaemic corn syrup. It's inspired by something I once bought from my local Japanese market – a cluster containing the usual nut and caramel combination, but with green tea powder, soy sauce and Japanese chilli crackers too! If you'd prefer to use ready-made popcorn, make sure it's plain (if you use lightly salted popcorn, omit the soy sauce). You won't be able to stop eating them!

SERVES 4

60 g/2 oz/⅓ cup popcorn kernels
+ 1½ tablespoons coconut oil or safflower oil, or 7 cups unsalted ready-made popcorn

175 g/6 oz/¾ cup melted margarine or ghee or coconut butter

115 g/4 oz/½ cup rice syrup

325 g/11 oz/1⅓ cups light brown sugar

½ teaspoon bicarbonate of soda (baking soda)

a little less than 1 teaspoon gluten-free soya sauce

100 g/3½ oz/¾ cup unsalted shelled peanuts (optional)

½ cup Mochi chilli crackers or a pinch of cayenne pepper

¼ teaspoon ground green tea powder

Prepare a tray lined with a silicon liner or well-oiled aluminum foil. Pop your kernels the usual way by heating the oil in a heavy saucepan and adding the corn. Once popped, set aside to cool.

Put the margarine or ghee, rice syrup and sugar into a heavy saucepan, stir, and bring to the boil over medium heat. Stop stirring and let it boil for about 10 minutes or until the temperature reaches 150°C/300°F on a sugar thermometer. Turn off the heat, add the bicarbonate of soda and soy sauce, stir, then add the popcorn, peanuts (if using) and crackers. Stir this quickly, as the syrup cools very fast and can harden. Pour the mixture onto the prepared tray and spread it quickly with a wooden spoon. Sprinkle with the green tea powder. Leave to cool, then crunch away!

To make a plain version of this, simply replace the soy sauce with ½ teaspoon of sea salt, omit the crackers and tea and reduce the margarine or ghee to 115 g/4 oz/½ cup.

Variations

Choc and Nut: Use a handful of chocolate chips and nuts instead of the Mochi chilli crackers.

Maple syrup: Swap the rice syrup for maple syrup.

Shortbread Cookies

Kids and adults love baking these cookies. Let your creative juices flow by cutting out this lovely dough in different shapes and icing them in fabulous natural colours.

MAKES 12

200 g/7 oz/1 cup margarine or coconut butter

85 g/3 oz/⅓ cup unrefined golden caster (superfine) sugar

1 teaspoon vanilla extract

200 g/7 oz/1½ cups gluten-free flour

60 g/2 oz/½ cup ground almonds

½ teaspoon xanthan gum

pinch of sea salt

Cream the margarine, sugar and vanilla extract with an electric whisk or in a KitchenAid (or other food mixer) until creamy and fluffy, about 2 minutes. Sift the remaining ingredients and add to the sugar mixture in one go. Fold the mixture until well blended using a wooden spoon or spatula, then wrap in clingfilm and leave to cool in the refrigerator for at least 1 hour.

Preheat the oven to 180°C/350°F/gas mark 4. Line a baking tray with a silicon liner, or get a non-stick baking tray ready. Flour the work surface and rolling pin. Knead the dough a couple of times and roll it out to about 0.5cm/¼ inch thick. Cut out the shapes you like and place them on the prepared tray.

Bake in the preheated oven for about 10–12 minutes or until very light in colour. You don't really want the cookies to colour much, or burn around the edges. Remove from the oven and let them cool slightly on the baking tray. Then remove on to a wire rack to cool completely before icing with Vegan Royal Icing Sugar (page 161). Store in an airtight container for up to two days.

2

little
miss
muffin

Good news! There are many **new ways** to make goodies just like the real thing, but without gluten, dairy or soy. Gone are the days of sawdust muffins and cardboard loaves. Gums such as xanthan or guar give you **light and fluffy** baked goods. You can buy or mix your own gluten-free flour to make fluffy **muffins and scones**. Or try maple-syrup-soaked pancakes and protein-rich loaves. You can even have **delicate cupcakes** with fabulous frostings. Just follow these simple steps: add **super grains** such as quinoa and flax meal to inject extra protein and essential fatty acids. **Fold** in gluten-free flour so as not to knock out carbon dioxide. Use **paper cake cases** so that muffins stay fresher for longer. Use **ice cream scoops** for portion control and even sizes – **smaller** muffins retain their moisture. **Freeze** them as soon as they cool. Thaw, then **flash** them briefly in the oven. More reason than ever to look forward to breakfast again!

Valrhona Chocolate and Orange Muffins

Muffins, like bread, are perfect in the sense that they are lower in fat than cakes yet seem to leave you feeling utterly satisfied. This holds especially true for this chocolate muffin. Although sometimes nothing beats the chocolate rush of a fudgey brownie, you can't really eat them that often since they are so rich. This muffin has a chocolatey dough, as well as decadent half-melted dark chocolate pieces inside which seem to ooze out as you bite into it. With orange pieces and a hint of Cointreau, it is pure indulgence. Have one for breakfast. Well, it is a muffin!

MAKES 12

70 g/2½ oz/5 tablespoons margarine or ghee or coconut butter

175 g/6 oz/1 cup dark chocolate, such as Valrhona or Green & Black's, chopped

150 ml/5 fl oz/⅔ cup rice or almond milk

zest and juice of ½ an orange

2 organic eggs

1 tablespoon Cointreau or Grand Marnier, (optional)

175 g/6 oz/1⅓ cups gluten-free flour

60 g/2 oz/⅓ cup light brown sugar

60 g/2 oz/½ cup cocoa powder

½ teaspoon xanthan gum

1½ teaspoons baking powder

½ teaspoon bicarbonate of soda (baking soda)

⅓ teaspoon sea salt

115 g/4 oz/⅔ cup candied orange peel

Preheat the oven to 200°C/400°F/gas mark 6. Place medium-sized paper cases in muffin tins or grease them lightly with a little oil or melted margarine.

Heat the margarine or ghee or coconut butter with half the chocolate, the milk and orange juice until smooth. Take off the heat and set aside. Let it cool slightly, then whisk in the eggs, orange zest and Cointreau (if using) until you have a smooth silky mixture with no visible lumps. Sift all the dry ingredients and add to the chocolate mixture. Blend in the rest of the chopped chocolate and the orange zest. Pour the mixture two-thirds of the way up the prepared muffin cases and bake in the preheated oven for about 15–18 minutes.

Skewer testing won't tell you much, as you may hit a chunk of chocolate. The muffin will rise beautifully and be springy to the touch. And fabulous on the tastebuds!

Banana Raisin Bread

This is a hearty and delectable cake that's perfect for breakfast, with coffee or afternoon tea. You can cut it into slices the following day and lightly toast them before spreading them with non-dairy butter. This recipe doubles as a muffin – just pour the mixture into prepared muffin cases and bake for about 15–18 minutes. It also freezes very well, so make a large batch and take them out as you need them.

SERVES 6–8

200 g/7 oz/1½ cups gluten-free flour

60 g/2 oz/½ cup buckwheat flour

1 teaspoon xanthan gum

1 teaspoon bicarbonate of soda (baking soda)

1 teaspoon baking powder

½ teaspoon cinnamon

½ teaspoon freshly grated nutmeg

½ teaspoon sea salt

2 large organic eggs

175 g/6 oz/1 cup demerara sugar

1½ teaspoon vanilla extract

115 ml/4 fl oz/¼ cup sunflower oil or melted coconut butter or light olive oil

3 medium bananas, mashed

4 tablespoons rice or almond milk

60 g/2 oz/½ cup walnuts, coarsely chopped

80 g/3 oz/½ cup raisins

Topping

2 tablespoons gluten-free flour

1 tablespoon margarine or ghee or coconut butter

85 g/3 oz/½ cup light brown sugar

1 teaspoon cinnamon

60 g/2 oz/½ cup walnuts, finely chopped

Preheat the oven to 180°C/350°F/gas mark 4. Lightly grease a 20 x 10 cm/8 x 4 inch loaf tin with some oil and set aside.

Make the topping by putting the flour into a bowl with the margarine or ghee or coconut butter, sugar and cinnamon and mix with your fingers until you have chunky crumbs. Add the walnuts and set aside.

Sift the flours with the xanthan gum, bicarbonate of soda, baking powder, spices and salt. In a separate bowl, mix the eggs, sugar and vanilla extract together, then add the oil, mashed banana and rice milk. Make a little well in the centre of the dry ingredients, add the banana mixture and then the walnuts and raisins. Mix with a wooden spoon and stop stirring as soon as everything is mixed in.

Pour the mixture into the prepared tin, spread evenly with the topping, pat down gently and bake for about 40–45 minutes or until a skewer inserted in the middle comes out clean. Leave the loaf in the tin for about 5 minutes after it comes out of the oven, then remove and place topping side up on a wire rack to cool completely before cutting.

Maple-sweetened Corn Muffins

These golden muffins are best fresh, but will still be moist the next day. Once you have mastered this basic recipe you can add different ingredients such as dried cranberries or walnuts, coconut flakes to make different muffins every time. For a savoury twist, you can even reduce the amount of sugar and serve them alongside a hearty chilli. Chop some jalapeños and toss them into the batter for a spicy alternative.

MAKES 12

130 g/4 oz/1 cup gluten-free flour mix

175 g/6 oz/1 cup cornmeal (yellow or blue) or polenta

½ teaspoon xanthan gum

3½ teaspoons baking powder

pinch of sea salt (optional)

115 g/4 oz/½ cup margarine or ghee or coconut butter, at room temperature

150 g/5 oz/⅔ cup maple sugar or unrefined golden caster (superfine) sugar

2 organic eggs, separated

1 teaspoon vanilla extract

225 g/8 fl oz/1 cup rice milk

Preheat the oven to 200°C/400°F/gas mark 6. Lightly grease a set of muffin tins – you will need enough for 12 muffins – and place in the oven.

Meanwhile, sift the flour, cornmeal, xanthan gum, baking powder and salt (if using) into a bowl. Set aside.

Cream the margarine or ghee or coconut butter with the sugar until light and fluffy. Add the yolks in stages and whisk for about 2–3 minutes. In a spotlessly clean bowl, whisk the egg whites until they are glossy and stiff.

Now, blend the vanilla extract and some of the rice milk into the yolk and margarine mixture, then continue by alternating with the flour mixture and so on until the batter is just mixed. Gently fold in the egg whites and immediately pour the batter into the prepared tin, up to about 1 cm/½ inch from the top edge. Place in the preheated oven for 25–30 minutes, until lightly browned.

Pumpkin Spice Muffins

Every time I make these muffins it feels like Christmas. They fill up the house with the most beautiful homely aroma. I haven't used a lot of sugar in this recipe – if it's not sweet enough for you, drizzle them with a little maple syrup as they come out of the oven. Heaven scent!

MAKES 12

200 g/7 oz/1½ cups gluten-free flour

1½ teaspoon bicarbonate of soda (baking soda)

1½ teaspoons baking powder

3½ teaspoons pumpkin spice or allspice

1 teaspoon xanthan gum

2 organic eggs

175 g/6 oz/½ cup honey or maple syrup

2 tablespoons molasses (sorghum or regular)

2 teaspoons fresh ginger, grated

1 teaspoon cider vinegar or plain vinegar

185 g/6½ oz/¾ cup unsweetened pumpkin purée (not pumpkin pie filling)

85 ml/3 fl oz/⅓ cup light olive oil or ghee or coconut butter, melted

60 g/2 oz/½ cup chopped walnuts

Preheat the oven to 180°C/350°F/gas mark 4. Place 12 paper cases in your muffin tin or grease lightly with a little oil.

Sift the dry ingredients together and set aside. Whisk the eggs with the honey or maple syrup and molasses. Add the ginger, vinegar, pumpkin purée and oil, and whisk to a smooth consistency. Blend in the flour mixture with the walnuts and pour into the muffin cases, leaving a little space below the rim so that the muffins have room to expand.

Bake in the preheated oven for about 20 minutes or until the muffins are golden and a skewer inserted in the centre comes out clean.

Breakfast Porridge

Along with rice pudding, porridge is the ultimate comfort food. Now you can enjoy porridge again with flakes made from buckwheat or rice, made to resemble regular oatflakes.

100 g/3½ oz/1 scant cups buckwheat or poha flakes

225 ml/8 fl oz rice or almond milk

3 teaspoons unrefined light brown sugar or maple syrup (optional)

pinch of sea salt

Stir the buckwheat or poha flakes with the rest of the ingredients over a medium low heat until thick and creamy, about 5–7 minutes. Pour into your favourite bowl and sprinkle with any of the following: a pinch of saffron, muscovado sugar, chocolate, maple syrup, honey, rice milk, coconut milk, sliced fruits and nuts or berries.

Divine Cupcakes

Cupcakes are the new cakes! Who doesn't like them? Cupcakes can turn a fully-grown adult into an over-excited kid. I've seen grown men jump up and down for them and uptight women swoon at the sight of these seemingly innocent cakes. They are so unassuming when they first come out of the oven. But let me tell you, once you dress them up, you will not recognize them any more. With the help of some wild frosting, sugar crystals and other decorations, they can be dressed up and even taken out around town. A complete makeover! You can bake one batch but use completely different frostings such as chocolate, lemon or berry to come up with fabulous mini-cakes. There is just something so adorable and heart-warming about cupcakes.

MAKES 50 SMALL CUPCAKES

225 ml/8 fl oz/1 cup rice milk or almond milk or carbonated water such as Perrier

4 large organic egg whites

400 g/13 oz/3 cups gluten-free flour

350 g/12 oz/1½ cups unrefined golden caster (superfine) sugar

1 teaspoon xanthan gum

4 teaspoons baking powder

pinch of sea salt

150 g/6 oz/²⁄₃ cup margarine or ghee or coconut butter

1 teaspoon vanilla extract

1½ teaspoons lemon zest, finely chopped

Preheat the oven to 180°C/350°F/gas mark 4. Line a small-sized muffin tin with paper cases.

Briefly whisk 85 ml/3 fl oz/⅓ cup of the rice milk or carbonated water and the egg whites together and set aside. Sift the flour, sugar, xanthan gum, baking powder and salt together and place in the bowl of a KitchenAid (or other food mixer) fitted with a paddle. Add the margarine or ghee and start whisking on medium speed. Add the vanilla extract, lemon zest and the rest of the rice milk, whisk for 1–2 minutes, then add the egg white mixture in stages and whisk for a further 10 seconds.

Pour the mixture into the paper cups and bake in the preheated oven for about 12–15 minutes or until a skewer inserted comes out clean. Leave to cool, then decorate with Dark Chocolate Ganache (page 144), or Vanilla Buttercream (page 155) or Frosting in a Flash (page 161) adding any other goodies you wish.

Variations

Remember that you can make cupcakes with almost any fluffy cake recipe in this book – Carrot Cake (pages 87, 88), Extra-virgin Olive Oil Cake (page 69), Might Coconut Muffins (page 52) etc.

Mighty Coconut Muffins

This recipe uses everything coconut. Virgin coconut oil, coconut milk, desiccated coconut. Virgin coconut oil is not hydrogenated, contains no trans-fatty acids and is high in lauric acid. You can even put it on your skin as a moisturizer! If you're feeling up to it, cover the cooled muffins with some coconut frosting.

MAKES 12

220 g/7 oz/1¾ cups gluten-free flour

40 g/1¼ oz/⅓ cup sweet rice flour (Mochiko)

2 teaspoons baking powder

1 teaspoon xanthan gum

dash of sea salt

2 organic eggs

225 ml/8 fl oz/1 cup coconut milk

1 teaspoon vanilla extract

175 ml/6 fl oz/¾ cup expeller-pressed 'virgin' coconut oil, melted and cooled

5 tablespoons unsweetened apple sauce

175 g/6 oz/¾ cup unrefined golden caster (superfine) sugar

85 g/3 oz/1 cup desiccated coconut

Preheat the oven to 190°C/375°F/gas mark 5. Prepare your muffin tins by lining them with paper cases. Make sure that all your ingredients, except for the coconut oil, are at room temperature before you begin.

Sift the flours, baking powder, xanthan gum and salt together into a bowl. In another bowl, lightly whisk the eggs and add the coconut milk, vanilla extract, coconut oil, apple sauce and sugar. Fold in the flour mixture, add the desiccated coconut and stir until smooth.

Pour the mixture into the prepared muffin cases and bake in the preheated oven for about 18–20 minutes or until a skewer inserted into the centre comes out clean.

Apple Hemp Seed Muffins

Hemp seeds and hemp oil are among the best sources of Omega-3 fatty acids in the vegetable kingdom. Hemp has the highest amount of protein of any food, after soya. But unlike soya, it is digested very well because it resembles the protein naturally found in humans. One handful of hemp seeds per day can supply adequate protein and essential oils for an adult! Besides the fact that it can grow virtually anywhere and with little or no chemical fertilizers, hemp also has a variety of end-products, such as paper, cosmetics, fuel, textiles, building materials, furniture and more – in fact the Chinese have been using it for ropes for over 5,000 years. Hemp seeds aren't for the birds any more!

MAKES 12

60 g/2 oz/½ cup brown rice

60 g/2 oz/½ cup sorghum flour

60 g/2 oz/½ cup tapioca flour

70 g/2½ oz/½ cup hulled hemp seeds

1 teaspoon ground cinnamon

1 teaspoon xanthan gum

2 teaspoons baking powder

½ teaspoon bicarbonate of soda (baking soda)

1 large organic egg

ground flax seeds (see page 12)

45 g/1½ oz/½ cup grated apples, unskinned

115 ml/4 fl oz/½ cup light olive oil or safflower oil or coconut oil

115 ml/4 fl oz/½ cup agave nectar or rice syrup

175 ml/6 fl oz/¾ cup rice or almond milk, mixed with 1 tablespoon lemon juice or cider vinegar

1 teaspoon vanilla extract

lemon zest to decorate

Preheat the oven to 190°C/375°F/gas mark 5. Place muffin cases in a muffin tin. Sift all the dry ingredients together into a large bowl, including the egg replacement if you're using it, and add the grated apple.

Mix the rest of the ingredients together until smooth and add to the dry mixture in one go. Stir until just mixed. Scoop the mixture into the muffin cases and bake in the preheated oven for about 15–20 minutes or until a skewer inserted into the centre comes out clean.

Decorate with a few strands of lemon zest.

Buckwheat and Chestnut Pancakes

The ancient Chinese used to make pancakes, and during the Middle Ages Europeans used to buy pre-made ones from food markets. Even cowboys were known to cook pancakes over campfires as a main meal. Indian dosas, Mexican tortillas, Ethiopian teff and Scottish oatcakes are all different variations. Chestnut flour, which gives these pancakes a lovely nutty taste, can easily be replaced with rice flour. This recipe can be used to make blinis by simply pouring smaller quantities into the pan to make smaller pancakes.

MAKES 8 LARGE PANCAKES

85 g/3 oz/¾ cup buckwheat flour

60 g/2 oz/½ cup chestnut flour, or brown rice flour

30 g/1 oz/¼ cup tapioca flour

1½ teaspoons baking powder

½ teaspoon bicarbonate of soda (baking soda)

2 organic eggs, yolks and whites separated + 1 extra egg white

350 ml/12 fl oz/1⅓–1½ cups rice milk or almond milk or coconut juice

1½ tablespoons olive oil or coconut butter, melted

½ teaspoon vanilla extract

pinch of sea salt

Sift the flours, baking powder and bicarbonate of soda together. Whisk the egg yolks, 225 ml/8 fl oz/1 cup of the rice milk, the oil and the vanilla extract together until smooth. Add the flours and blend just until homogenous. Add up to 115 ml/4 fl oz/½ cup more rice milk if you prefer thinner pancakes.

Whisk the egg whites with a pinch of sea salt until stiff peaks form, and gently fold into the batter.

Heat a non-stick frying pan with a little oil and pour in the batter about ¼ inch thick, or enough to make the size of pancake you wish, and as soon as it the top starts bubbling and the sides become golden, flip it over and cook for a couple of minutes. The first pancake is never pretty, as the pan isn't at the right temperature, so drizzle it with some maple syrup and quietly eat it yourself!

Pistachio and Raspberry Financiers

In this case, the word 'financiers' doesn't mean people in suits running around investing in companies! Although some people do say these cakes were given this curious name during the time when butter and almonds were very expensive and only rich financiers could afford to eat them. They're light, moist cakes, and very pretty studded with juicy red raspberries. They can be made in various flavours, such as dried currant, chocolate, lemon or even plain. I pour a little syrup on top as they come out of the oven so that they're still moist next day, but you can omit this step if you'll be eating them on the day they are baked. They can also be baked in little moulds and served as petit fours.

MAKES 18–20 MINI FINANCIERS

100 g/3½ oz/½ cup equal parts ground almonds and unrefined golden caster (superfine) sugar

65 g/2 oz/½ cup gluten-free flour

4 tablespoons raw almond paste (not butter)

3 tablespoons pistachio paste

green spinach colouring

115 g/4 oz/1 cup melted and cooled ghee or margarine or coconut butter

150 g/5 oz/5 organic egg whites

70 g/2½ oz/²⁄₃ cup icing (confectioners') sugar

24 raspberries

1 tablespoon Simple Syrup (page 158)

Preheat the oven to 220°C/425°F/gas mark 7. Prepare silicon or muffin moulds.

Mix together the almond/sugar mix and the flour and set aside. In a KitchenAid (or other food mixer) fitted with a paddle attachment, or using a wooden spoon, mix together the two pastes, the melted ghee or margerine or coconut butter and the green colouring until well blended. Add the dry ingredients and mix thoroughly.

Whisk the egg whites with the icing sugar until stiff and glossy, and fold gently into the green mixture. Spoon the mixture into the prepared moulds to come two-thirds of the way up the sides, then drop in one or two raspberries and push them down with your fingers. Bake in the preheated oven for about 15–20 minutes or until they look puffed and light golden. Flip the hot financiers out of the moulds as soon as they come out of the oven and pour a tablespoon of simple syrup over the top.

Leave them to cool before serving. Store in an airtight container for up to three days, or frozen for up to three weeks.

Proper Scones

My mother-in-law, Jean, came up with this recipe when she heard I was working on this book. She is an amazing baker and loves to make all sorts of desserts, but keeps her figure trim by playing 18 holes of golf every other day. Wish I had that discipline! You can add all sorts of goodies to the dough, such as cocoa powder and chocolate chips, cranberries and orange zest, and even lemon and hemp seeds. There's nothing like livening up an old favourite like this with an unusual ingredient.

MAKES 6–8

220 g/7 oz/1¾ cups gluten-free flour

1½ teaspoons baking powder

1½ teaspoons bicarbonate of soda (baking soda)

60 g/2 oz/½ cup ground almonds

½ teaspoon xanthan gum

pinch of sea salt

85 g/3 oz/⅓ cup unrefined golden caster (superfine) sugar

85 g/3 oz/⅓ cup margarine or ghee or coconut butter

2 large organic eggs, plus extra for brushing

85 g/3 oz/½ cup raisins

Preheat the oven to 220°C/425°F/gas mark 7. Line a baking tray with lightly greased and floured parchment paper.

Sift the flour, baking powder, bicarbonate of soda, ground almonds, xanthan gum, salt and sugar together. Rub the margarine into the flour mixture until you have a texture like large breadcrumbs. Lightly beat the eggs, add the raisins, and mix into the dough. Wrap the dough with clingfilm and let it rest in the fridge for 1 hour or more.

Lightly flour the work surface and quickly roll out the dough about 6 cm/2½ inches thick. If you feel it warming up as you handle it, put it back in the fridge for a few minutes to let it firm up again. Stamp out rounds with a pastry cutter and place on the prepared tray. Lightly brush the tops twice with a little egg wash and bake in the preheated oven for about 12 minutes or until golden.

Remove from the oven and transfer to a cooling rack. These are best eaten while still slightly warm from the oven, spread with a little Mock Whipped Cream (page 148) and jam.

3

bake your cake

You may need to unlearn everything you ever knew about baking. Gluten- and dairy-free cakes and tarts are slightly different in texture and taste but are just as yummy. Don't be afraid to try them out. They are so **easy to prepare**. First master the simple yet versatile Sponge Cake and then move on to making other equally simple cakes. **Layer** them with **buttercream**, soak them generously with **syrups**, assemble them with lots of luscious Mock Whipped Cream, dress them up with **fresh fruits**, decorate them with anything pretty. Play around with them. You'll forget they're gluten- and dairy-free. **Sprinkle** with icing sugar, top them with bright frostings, **display** them on a cake stand and serve them on your best china. Now bake your cake… and eat it!

Le Fraisier

This is by far one of the prettiest cakes around. I wrote an article for a food magazine about this cake and got so carried away you'd think I'd written a love letter! Its layers and bright red strawberries make you think of an eighteenth-century tea party in the French countryside, or a pretty summer dress. The combination of the cake moistened with kirsch, sweet tart strawberries and light vanilla-studded pastry cream, is not only divine but perfectly balanced.

SERVES 4–6

1 x 20 cm/8 inch Classic Genoise (page 68) or Sponge Cake (page 65)

½ x recipe Crème Mousseline (page 146)

6 strawberrries, halved

Syrup

1 tablespoon unrefined light sugar

200 ml/7 fl oz/1 cup water

4 tablespoons kirsch

Reserve one strawberry for the decoration. Cut the strawberries in half. You want them to be pretty much the same size. Set aside.

The cake can be baked in either a square or a round tin. Cut the outer edges off the cooked and cooled cake. Try not to remove too much, just the hard crusty bits. Cut the cake evenly in half horizontally and place the bottom half into a 20 x 2.5cm/8 x 1 inch springform cake tin or flan case or ring.

To make the syrup, boil the water and sugar together in a pan for 1 minute. Allow to cool, then add the kirsch. Using a pastry brush, brush the cake with the kirsch syrup. Be generous – it may at first seem like too much syrup but, as you'll soon see, the cake soaks it all up.

Spoon the crème mousseline into a piping bag and, starting in the middle and moving outwards, pipe the cream in a continuous circle until you get to the edge of the cake. You may have a tiny bit of cream left over which you won't use. Place the strawberry halves in a single layer all over the top of the crème mousseline. The best way to do this is to choose the best and most uniform ones first and place the cut sides against the cake ring. That way, once it's cut you'll be able to see the berries all lined up around the edge of the cake. Then fill the rest of the cake with the remaining strawberries.

Take the other half of the cake and slice across the top so that it's level. Brush one side generously with syrup and place on top of the strawberries, inside the ring. Gently push the cake down a little, cover with clingfilm and refrigerate for a minimum of 1 hour.

Decorate with the reserved strawberry cut in half, gold leaves, or anything you fancy. Just remember to keep it simple. Remove the cake ring and serve.

Variations

If you like, you can roll out a thin layer of store-bought marzipan and cover the top of the cake with it, being careful to cut it to the right size. Then decorate with icing sugar or pipe cream on top. Other decorations you could choose are: almond paste, chocolate décor, apricot glaze, Italian meringue and fresh strawberries.

Sponge Cake

This is the one of the easiest, most versatile cakes you can bake. It can be layered with Mock Whipped Cream and fruits or soaked with syrup and assembled as a glorious cake layered with Vanilla Buttercream.

SERVES 6

60 g/2 oz/¼ cup margarine or ghee or coconut butter, melted at room temperature

4 organic eggs, separated

115 g/4 oz/½ cup unrefined golden caster (superfine) sugar

1 teaspoon vanilla extract

zest of 1 small lemon, finely chopped

130 g/4 oz/1 cup gluten-free flour

pinch of sea salt

1 teaspoon baking powder

1 teaspoon xanthan gum

Preheat the oven to 180°C/350°F/gas mark 4. Grease a 20 cm/8 inch cake tin and set aside.

Whisk the yolks and sugar together until the mixture drips like ribbons from the spoon, about 10 minutes. Add the vanilla extract and lemon zest and beat again to incorporate. Meanwhile, sift the flour, salt, baking powder and xanthan gum together. Fold into the egg yolk mixture. Whisk the egg whites until stiff and fluffy. Gradually fold the whites into the flour and add the melted margarine or ghee. Try to mix gently and as little as possible.

Pour into the cake tin and bake in the preheated oven for about 30–40 minutes, or until a skewer inserted in the middle comes out clean. Remove the cake from the cake tin and flip on to a wire rack to cool. You can also make the cake in two sandwich tins, in which case bake for only 20 minutes.

You can replace 30 g/1 oz/¼ cup of the flour with good-quality cocoa powder for a chocolatey effect!

Basic Tart Dough

MAKES 1 X 20–23 CM/8–9 INCH TART BASE

2 organic egg yolks

½ teaspoon vanilla extract

1½ teaspoons chilled water or rice milk

150 g/5 oz/1¼ cups gluten-free flour

30 g/1 oz/¼ cup icing (confectioners') sugar

1½ teaspoons xanthan gum

85 g/3 oz/⅓ cup chilled margarine, cut into cubes

1 teaspoon finely chopped lemon zest

pinch of sea salt

Blend together the egg yolks, vanilla extract and water. Sift the flour and sugar, and then add the xanthan gum, margarine, lemon zest and salt in a KitchenAid (or other food mixer) fitted with a paddle attachment. The mixture will resemble coarse breadcrumbs. With the machine running, add the egg and water mixture until a dough forms. Wrap the dough in clingfilm and refrigerate for at least 2 hours.

Preheat the oven to 190°C/375°F/gas mark 5. Roll the dough out on a floured board and line a 20 cm/8 inch flan tin with it. Although gluten-free dough does not really rise, gently prick the bottom of the dough with a fork. Bake in the preheated oven for about 18–20 minutes or until golden.

Pink Peach and Quinoa Crumble

The colour from the peaches and their skin make this crumble a lovely pinkish colour. This crumble calls for quinoa, buckwheat or poha (rice) flakes – or you can simply open a bag of gluten-free muesli. It's a light, delicate dessert that can be made with any fruits you fancy or happen to have around. Try a tropical crumble with mangoes, pineapples and bananas. Douse with a splash of rum or Malibu, add some coconut flakes to the topping, and serve with some cool Lemongrass and Coconut Sorbet (page 118). I like to serve this yummy dessert with some lovely vanilla Crème Anglaise (page 147).

SERVES 4–6

500 g/1 lb 2 oz peaches, sliced 5 cm/2 inches thick

85 g/3 oz/⅓ cup unrefined golden caster (superfine) sugar

½ teaspoon vanilla extract

130 g/4 oz/scant 1 cup gluten-free flour

60 g/2 oz/¼ cup margarine or ghee or coconut butter, plus 1 tablespoon extra

60 g/2 oz/⅓ cup muscovado sugar

85 g/3 oz/¾ cups gluten-free muesli or 60 g/2 oz/½ cups quinoa, buckwheat or poha flakes

2 tablespoons hazelnuts, chopped roughly

pinch of nutmeg

⅓ teaspoon ground cinnamon

Preheat the oven to 200°C/400°F/gas mark 6.

Put the peaches into a very hot frying pan with the caster sugar and vanilla and sear on both sides for about 3 minutes. They will be caramelized and a bit soft but will still hold their shape. In a food processor or KitchenAid (or other food mixer), pulse or mix the flour and the margarine or ghee until large crumbs form. Add the muscovado sugar, muesli, hazelnuts, nutmeg and cinnamon and mix a bit more until it all comes together but it's not in clumps – what you're looking for is large airy crumbs.

Spread the peach slices in individual ramekins or a large ovenproof dish, and lightly sprinkle the crumble on top without pushing the mixture down on to the fruits. Place in the preheated oven and bake for about 15–20 minutes or until golden, bubbly and downright delicious.

Classic Genoise

Who would have thought that the great Genoise could be converted into a gluten-free cake while still retaining its elevated status? Master this cake and you can make any cake recipe in the world. Created in Genoa, the Genoise soon became known as the mother of all French cakes. It does not use chemical leaveners, only eggs and air, and uses very little fat. Sturdy yet extremely airy, it is an all-purpose cake that, if made successfully, never fails to deliver. It can be layered with Vanilla Buttercream (page 155) or jam and sprinkled with icing sugar, or dressed up more elaborately with Crème Patissèrie (page 146), mousses and mousselines. The Genoise is the perfect cake for Simple Syrup (page 158), as it absorbs the sweet liquid without falling apart.

MAKES A 20–23 CM/8–9 INCH TART

20 g/¾ oz/4 tablespoons margarine or ghee

1 teaspoon vanilla extract

zest of 1 small lemon

130 g/4 oz/1 cup gluten-free flour

1 teaspoon xanthan gum

4 organic eggs

120 g/4 oz/1 cup unrefined golden caster (superfine) sugar

Preheat the oven to 180°C/350°F/gas mark 4. Take a 20 cm/8 inch cake tin and lightly grease it with some melted margarine or ghee.

Melt the margarine or ghee with the vanilla and the lemon zest, then set aside to cool. Sift the flour with the xanthan gum and set aside. In a KitchenAid (or other food mixer) bowl, whisk together the eggs and sugar until pale, about 1 minute. Place the bowl over a pan of simmering water and, using a balloon whisk or electric whisk, vigorously whisk the mixture until frothy and pale, about 5 minutes. Take off the heat, put the bowl back on the machine, and add the whisk attachment. You now need to cool the mixture as well as adding more volume to it. Start the machine on high and whisk the mixture for about 10 minutes, until very pale and creamy and about 3 times its original volume, or until ribbon stage. The mixture will be cool to the touch.

At this stage you'll need to work quite quickly. Take 2 tablespoons of the mixture and whisk it into the melted margarine or ghee. Quickly fold the flour into the egg mixture in 3 additions, then fold in the margarine. The mixture will fall slightly but don't worry, just keep working quickly. Pour it into the prepared tin and bake in the preheated oven for about 20–25 minutes or until a skewer inserted in the middle comes out clean. Refrain from opening the oven for the first 15 minutes as this may affect the rise of the cake. Let the cake cool for a good 3–4 minutes before flipping it onto a wire rack. Allow it to cool completely before cutting.

Variations

Chocolate Genoise Simply replace 60 g/2 oz/½ cup of the flour with unsweetened cocoa powder.

Extra-virgin Olive Oil Lemon Cake

For olive oil lovers everywhere, this cake is pure Mediterranean, with its olive oil, lemons and toasted pinenuts. It's made with pure extra-virgin olive oil, high in beneficial antioxidants – use an oil that has a mild taste, not a strong one, as it will really affect the end result. If you are lucky enough to get Meyer lemons, use them. But the cake is just as good with regular juicy lemons. You can replace the chestnut flour with gluten-free flour if you're having a hard time obtaining it. See Top Sites and Addresses (page 184) for online orders.

SERVES 6–8

130 g/4 oz/1 cup gluten-free flour

35 g/1¼ oz/⅓ cup chestnut flour

60 g/2 oz/½ cup ground almonds

1 teaspoon xanthan gum

2 teaspoons baking powder

pinch of sea salt

225 g/8 oz/1 cup unrefined golden caster (superfine) sugar

juice of 1 large lemon and its zest, finely chopped

4 organic eggs

85 ml/3 fl oz/⅓ cup rice or almond milk

150 ml/5 fl oz/⅔ cup extra virgin olive oil

5 tablespoons margarine or ghee, melted and cooled

60 g/2 oz/½ cup lightly toasted pinenuts

Preheat the oven to 180°C/350°F/gas mark 4. Grease a 23 cm/9 inch cake tin with a little olive oil and set aside.

Sift the flours with the ground almonds, xanthan gum, baking powder and salt and set aside. In a KitchenAid (or other food mixer) fitted with a whisk attachment, whisk the sugar with the lemon zest for a minute or so to release the lemon's natural oils. Add the eggs and beat until pale and creamy, about 3 minutes, stopping the machine to scrape the mixture down the sides when necessary. With the machine running on low, add the rice or almond milk, olive oil and margarine or ghee. Gently fold in the flour mixture until just mixed and finally add the lemon juice and pinenuts.

Pour the mixture into the prepared tin and bake in the preheated oven for about 30–40 minutes or until a skewer inserted in the middle comes out clean. Flip the cake out of its tin and on to a wire rack to cool. You can serve this cake with chestnut purée, Luscious Lemon Cream (page 152) or fresh berries.

Luscious Fruit Tart

I think people who choose fruit tarts for dessert are quite wise. They're mainly eating fresh fruits, with a little creamy vanilla custard and a small amount of pastry crust. This is another recipe that you'd never guess was dairy- and gluten-free. There's only one rule, which is to assemble it at the last minute so that the pastry stays crisp and short.

SERVES 6–8

1 x Basic Tart Dough, in its tin (page 65)

½ quantity (or less depending on the size of the shell) Crème Patissèrie or Crème Mousseline (page 146)

fresh fruits of your choice

store-bought glaze or 115 g/4 oz/⅓ cup apricot jam

Keep the pastry case in its tin while you decorate. I like to use a piping bag for filling the pastry case with Crème Patissèrie/Mousseline - it's easier and keeps the cream level. But you can simply spoon in the cream and level it off with a spatula. Try not to have more than 2.5cm/1 inch or so of cream at the base of the shell. Decorate with whatever sliced fruit you like: strawberries, raspberries, pineapple, grapes, figs, plums, kiwis… Stay clear of melons, though, as they are too watery, and also of bananas, apples and pears, which tend to go brown quickly even with a glaze. Cut the fruits with a sharp knife – some can even be stamped out with small cookie or dough cutters.

Glaze your tart no matter what. It will keep the fruits fresh and add a shine and sparkle to your tart like you will not believe. If you haven't any store-bought glaze, thin out the apricot jam with 2–3 tablespoons water. Heat the mixture to boiling and take it off the heat. Whisk out any lumps with a fork and immediately brush the fruits with the warm glaze.

Brush the fruits only once, thinly, otherwise they'll be too gooey-looking. Pretend you're applying eyeshadow with a brush or painting with watercolour. That's how thinly and gently they need to be glazed. If you are using raspberries, don't brush them with jam as they don't glaze well.

There are several tricks you can use to decorate your fruit tart. Dot the surface with boysenberries for added colour. Split a vanilla pod in half, lightly moisten it with some water and roll it quickly in some caster sugar. Place on top of the tart with a strawberry cut in half. Try putting a small amount of gold or silver leaves on the surface – it elevates the tart instantly. Remove the tart from its pan just before serving.

LEMON TART SERVES 6–8

1 x Basic Tart Dough, in its tin (page 65)

1 x recipe Luscious Lemon Cream (page 152)

store-bought glaze

Fill the tart with the lemon cream and smooth the surface with a spatula. Top with store-bought glaze and remove from the tin at the last minute. Decorate with a few thin swirls of lemon zest or gold leaf. You could even sprinkle light brown sugar over the top and use a cook's torch to caramelize the tart.

L'Opéra

This classic French cake has six layers: joconde soaked in coffee syrup, chocolate ganache, coffee buttercream and smooth chocolate glaze. Although it has many layers it is surprisingly thin and elegant, just under 5 cm/2 inches high. You'll need to chill the cake during assembly, so make room for it in your refrigerator or freezer. This recipe, from my days at Cordon Bleu, makes quite a large Opéra, but you can cut it in half and freeze it.

SERVES 6–8

Joconde
150 g/5 oz/x cups ground almonds

45 g/1½ oz/⅓ cup gluten-free flour

115 g/4 oz/1 cup icing (confectioners') sugar

4 organic egg whites

60 g/2 oz/¼ cup unrefined golden granulated sugar

4 organic eggs, separated

2 tablespoons margarine or ghee or coconut butter, melted and cooled

2 x recipe Dark Chocolate Ganache (page 144)

1 x recipe Coffee Buttercream (page 155)

1 x recipe Coffee Simple Syrup (page 158)

Preheat the oven to 220°C/425°F/gas mark 7. Line two 30 x 20 cm/12 x 8 inch swiss roll trays with baking parchment, lightly brushed with melted coconut butter or ghee.

Sift the ground almonds, flour and icing sugar into a bowl and set aside. In a KitchenAid (or other food mixer) fitted with a whisk attachment, whisk all the egg whites until foamy then add the granulated sugar in stages until you get stiff peaks. Set aside. Whisk the egg yolks until pale and creamy, about 3 minutes. Fold in the flour mixture until just incorporated, then mix in the melted margarine, ghee or coconut butter. Fold in the meringue, making sure not to over-blend. Spread on to the prepared trays with a spatula. The best way to do this is to pour the lot into the middle of the tray, spread it in an X to the four corners of the tray, then fill in the gaps. Bake in the preheated oven for about 5–7 minutes only or until golden. Turn the tray on to a clean piece of baking parchment. Remove the tray but don't peel the papers off. Leave to cool, then trim and cut the cake to make two 25 cm/10 inch squares and 2 smaller pieces that can be joined together to make a third, and place in the freezer for about 15 minutes. This is to ensure that the cake remains firm and does not crumble under the weight of the syrup and buttercream.

Now, prepare your syrup, pastry brush, ganache, buttercream and spatula. Soak a slice of cake with some syrup, then spread with ⅔ of the buttercream. Soak another layer of cake, flip syrup side down on the first layer, and remove the parchment. Spread the top evenly with the ganache. Soak the last layer of cake and lay it on top, removing the parchment. Spread with the remaining buttercream and place the cake in the refrigerator or freezer while you prepare a chocolate glaze.

Melt 115 g/4 oz of chocolate in a microwave or a bowl over simmering water. Stir in 85 g/3 oz/⅓ cup of ghee, coconut butter or margarine. Place the cold cake on a cooling rack with a clean baking tray underneath. Pour the glaze on top and, with lightning speed, spread it evenly around. Tap the rack a few times, then cool the cake in the freezer or refrigerator. It freezes extremely well in an airtight container. Serve the cake chilled and cut it with a very sharp knife. On top you can write Opéra, as they do in the patisséries, or lay a simple edible gold leaf.

Lemon Pound Cake with an Orange Basil Glaze

This is a moist and intensely lemony cake that everyone loves. You could pour the mixture into muffin cases and bake mini-cakes instead, for about 15–20 minutes, depending on the size of your tins.

MAKES 2 LOAVES

325 g/11 oz/2½ cups gluten-free flour

60 g/2 oz/½ cup sweet rice flour

1 teaspoon xanthan gum

½ teaspoon bicarbonate of soda (baking soda)

½ teaspoon baking powder

pinch of sea salt

finely chopped zest 3 large lemons

400 g/14 oz/1¾ cup unrefined granulated sugar

225 g/8 oz/1 cup margarine or ghee

4 large organic eggs

1 teaspoon vanilla extract

85 ml/3 fl oz/⅓ cup fresh lemon juice

85 ml/3 fl oz/⅓ cup rice or almond milk

4 tablespoons unsweetened apple purée

150 ml/5 fl oz/⅔ cup light coconut milk

For the syrup

150 ml/5 fl oz/⅔ cup freshly squeezed orange juice

60 g/2 fl oz/½ cup unrefined golden caster (superfine) sugar

4 or 5 fresh basil leaves, torn

Preheat the oven to 180°C/350°F/gas mark 4. Lightly oil two 20 cm/8 inch loaf tins and set aside. Sift the flours, xanthan gum, bicarbonate of soda and baking powder together with a pinch of salt.

Make the syrup by boiling the orange juice and sugar with the basil over medium heat for about 3–4 minutes, then cover, remove from the heat and let it infuse.

Finely chop the lemon zest and place in a large bowl with the sugar and rub them between your fingers to release the natural lemon oils. In a KitchenAid (or other food mixer) fitted with a paddle attachment, cream the ghee or margarine with the citrus sugar until pale and creamy. Whisk the eggs and vanilla with a fork and add to the mixture in stages, scraping down the sides of the bowl if you need to. Blend in the lemon juice, rice milk, apple purée and light coconut milk. Add the sifted flour and the liquid alternately to the egg and sugar mixture, making sure to finish with the flour. Try not to over-mix. Pour the mixture into the prepared loaf tins and bake in the oven for about 50–60 minutes or until a skewer inserted into the centre comes out clean.

Take the loaves out of the oven and let them cool for about 10–12 minutes. Flip them on to a wire rack and remove the tins. Remove the basil leaves from the warm syrup and pour it all over the bottom of the loaves. Allow the loaves to cool completely before flipping it back up again.

Make a glaze by whisking about 300 g/10 oz/2½ cups of unrefined golden icing (confectioners') sugar with 4 tablespoons of lemon juice. Pour the glaze on top of the loaves and let them set before slicing. Remember, with all gluten-free cakes it's best to cut slices as you need them so that the left-over cake doesn't dry up.

Fudgey Hazelnut Brownies

Rich decadent chocolate squares with an adult edge! If you're allergic to nuts, omit the hazelnuts and replace half the amount with more chocolate chips. I love to add coffee extract and candied orange peel to the mixture. Sun-dried sour cherries and pistachios also work really well. Whatever you do, don't overbake them so they stay fudgey.

MAKES 9 CHUNKY SQUARES

175 g/6 oz dark (bittersweet) chocolate, diced

115 g/4 oz/½ cup margarine or ghee or coconut butter

100 g/3½ oz/¾ cup gluten-free flour

30 g/1 oz/¼ cup sweet rice flour (mochiko flour)

4 tablespoons cocoa powder

1 teaspoon xanthan gum

¼ teaspoon bicarbonate of soda (baking soda)

½ teaspoon baking powder

pinch of sea salt

115 g/4 oz/1 cup chopped hazelnuts, skinned and lightly roasted

85 g/3 oz/½ cup dark (bittersweet) chocolate chips

4 large organic eggs

300 g/10 oz/1¼ cups unrefined golden caster (superfine) sugar

2 teaspoons vanilla extract

1 tablespoon hazelnut oil

Preheat the oven to 180°C/360°F/gas mark 4. Line a 23 cm/9 inch square baking tin with two pieces of greased baking parchment. Lay the first piece horizontally in the tin, overlapping each end, then lay the second piece at right angles to it, so that the paper is criss-crossed. This will make it easier to remove the brownies after baking.

Place the chocolate and margarine or ghee in a bain-marie or microwave and stir it around a bit. Let it melt almost completely, then remove and let it cool down. The remaining bits of chocolate will continue to melt in the hot mixture.

Sift the flours, cocoa powder, xanthan gum, bicarbonate of soda and baking powder into a large bowl and add a pinch of salt. Stir in the hazelnuts and chocolate chips.

Put the eggs, sugar, vanilla extract and oil into another bowl and blend in the liquid chocolate mixture. Now add this mixture to the dry ingredients.

Pour the mixture into the prepared tin and bake in the preheated oven for about 30–40 minutes or until a skewer inserted into the centre comes out with just a few crumbs adhering to it. It will be crumbly until fully cooled, so try to resist cutting it until it's cooled down. Cut the brownies as you like them, in mini squares or serious chunky tiles.

White Chocolate Mochi Cake

Traditional mochi cakes are made with glutinous rice, which is pounded, mixed with various pastes and moulded into different shapes. Variants of mochi appear in every Asian culture from Chinese and Thai to Hawaiian and Filipino. This is a Hawaiianized Japanese cake that's soft and tender with the addition of eggs, chocolate and baking powder. I've added gluten-free flour and xanthan gum, which makes it fluffy, unlike other butter mochi cakes which rely solely on sweet rice flour and tend to be too gooey for the western palate. The white chocolate used in this recipe is dairy-free (yey!) but does contain soya lecithin. You can substitute dark chocolate for a deep cocoa version. Bake it with dried cherries for a sweet tangy taste, or simply make it plain. The mochiko flour, also known as sweet rice flour or glutinous rice flour, gives this cake a tender, slightly chewy texture that's utterly scrumptious and keeps moist for several days.

MAKES 12 SMALL OR 9 LARGE SQUARES

225 g/8oz /1 cup margarine or ghee or coconut butter

100 g/3½ oz/⅔ cup Oppenheimer white chocolate chips or chopped dark chocolate

90 g/3 oz/⅔ cup gluten-free flour

35 g/1½ oz/⅓ cup sweet rice flour (Mochiko)

½ teapoon xanthan gum

pinch of sea salt

1 teaspoon baking powder

85 g/3 oz/⅔ cup powdered unsweetened coconut

6 organic eggs

400 g/14 oz/1¾ cups unrefined golden caster (superfine) sugar

2 teaspoons vanilla extract

150 g/5 oz/1 cup chopped dried sour cherries

Preheat the oven to 160°C/325°F/gas mark 3. Line a 23 or 25 cm/9 or 10 inch square cake tin with baking parchment on both sides, like you would do for brownies.

Melt the margarine or ghee or coconut butter with the chocolate in a bowl set over simmering water or in a microwave until melted and smooth. Set aside to cool slightly.

Sift the flours, xanthan gum, salt, baking powder and powdered unsweetened coconut together.

Whisk the eggs, sugar and vanilla extract together until blended and add the chocolate mixture. Stir to mix the ingredients and then add the flour mixture and blend in with a whisk or spoon until smooth. Finally, add the sour cherries.

Pour into the prepared tin and bake in the preheated oven for about 40 minutes or until a skewer inserted in the middle comes out clean. The cake will rise, then fall slightly as it cools.

Let it cool completely before taking it out of the tin and cutting it into squares.

Silky Smooth Pumpkin Pie

Good old unfailing pumpkin pie! Who would have thought it could be this luscious and creamy without the use of any dairy? Simply par-bake a 23 cm/9 inch pastry case (see Basic Tart Dough page 65) until very light in colour, about 10 minutes, or a cream cracker crust (see Uncheesecake page 86). While it's cooling in the pan, assemble the filling. I like to use ready-cooked pumpkin from a can or jar, as it is so much easier, however if you prefer to make this yourself, see the recipe below. The rice syrup can be replaced with pure maple syrup, which goes wonderfully well with pumpkin. Top it with some Mock Whipped Cream (page 148)… in fact I'm having a slice as we speak!

SERVES 6–8

1 x Basic Tart Dough (page 65), baked for 10 minutes

3 organic eggs

85 g/3 oz/½ cup light brown sugar

1 teaspoon ground ginger

2 teaspoons vanilla extract

350 ml/12 fl oz/1½ cups coconut milk

400 g/14 oz/1½ cups unsweetened pumpkin purée

115 ml/4 fl oz/⅓ cup rice syrup or maple syrup

⅓ teaspoon sea salt

2 teaspoons gound allspice

Preheat the oven to 180°C/350°F/gas mark 4. In a large bowl, mix together the eggs, sugar, ground ginger, vanilla extract and coconut milk. Stir in the pumpkin purée, then add the rice or maple syrup, sea salt and allspice and stir until smooth. Pour the pumpkin mixture into the par-baked pastry case, still in its tin, and bake in the preheated oven for about 35–40 minutes or until it jiggles just slightly in the centre when gently shaken.

Let it cool completely, about 2–3 hours, preferably overnight (I know, it's a long time to wait!), before taking it out of the tin and serving.

PUMPKIN PUREE MAKES APPROX 500 G/1 LB/2 CUPS

Preheat the oven to 180°C/350°F/gas mark 4. Take a small pumpkin (roughly 3.5 kilos/7 lbs in weight) cut in half and remove the seeds and strigy fibres. Place the halves flesh side down in an ovenproof dish with 100 ml/3½ fl oz/1 cup of filtered water. Bake in the oven for 1 hour or until tender.

When cooked, remove from the dish and allow to cool completely. Once cool, scrap out the soft flesh and purée in a blender or food processor.

Molten Chocolate Cake

This is the kind of dessert you eat in restaurants and never imagine being able to make at home. Well, this recipe is going to change all that. In fact, it is so simple that once you get the hang of it, it may become your signature dessert!

The combination of dark chocolate and red wine is spectacular. It's two fantastic flavours and sensations in one. Cool heady sorbet with warm chocolate heaven. I came up with a sorbet recipe to go with the classic molten cake for a food show in Johannesburg (Cabernet Sauvignon Red Wine Gelato page 116). I used a Cape Town Cabernet Sauvignon, but feel free to use any red wine that's available.

SERVES 5

70 g/2½ oz/½ cup chopped dark (bittersweet) chocolate (minimum 70% cocoa solids)

115 g/4 oz/½ cup margarine or ghee or coconut butter

2 organic eggs

2 organic egg yolks

60 g/2 oz/¼ cup unrefined golden caster (superfine) sugar

2 teaspoons gluten-free flour

1 teaspoon vanilla extract

Preheat your oven to 200°C/400°F/gas mark 6. Take 5 ramekins 5 x ½ cm/2 x ¼ inches in size, butter them and dust with flour. Put the chocolate and margarine or ghee in a bowl and place in a bain-marie or a microwave until almost all the chocolate has melted. The heat of the bowl and the liquid chocolate will melt the rest while you're preparing the rest of the recipe. You also don't want it to be too hot, since you'll then have to wait for it to cool slightly before adding the eggs.

Whisk the eggs, yolks and sugar until pale and creamy and doubled in size. Pour the warm chocolate over the egg mixture, add the flour and vanilla extract, and blend until just combined. Do not over-mix. Quickly pour into the prepared ramekins and bake in the preheated oven for around 7–8 minutes. The sides will be set but the middle will remain soft and shiny. Serve immediately.

Martha's Moist Vegan Chocolate Cake

This is adapted from a recipe given to me by a dear friend, Martha Rosenthal, from Vermont. She bakes with so much love that you can almost taste it in her food. This cake is American-huge, moist, chocolatey and downright spectacular. You can easily halve the ingredients if you like, to make a smaller one. The frosting is virtually fat-free but you'd never guess – it's creamy and luscious, helped in part by the agar agar. You can also use the no-bake Frosting in a Flash (page 161), or glaze it with Dark Chocolate Ganache (page 144) for a different look with a smooth shiny finish. Either way, you'll find yourself cutting one too many slices.

SERVES 6–8

455 g/14½ oz/3½ cups gluten-free flour

60 g/2 oz/½ cup sweet rice flour (Mochiko)

1 tablespoon baking powder, plus 1 teaspoon

2 teaspoons bicarbonate of soda (baking soda)

115 g/4 oz/1 cup cocoa powder

2 teaspoons ground cinnamon

1½ teaspoons xanthan gum

225 ml/8 fl oz/1 cup light-tasting olive oil

950 ml/33 fl oz/3 cups maple syrup

2 teaspoons apple cider vinegar or lemon juice

4 teaspoons vanilla extract

450 ml/16 fl oz/2 cups filtered water or coconut juice

1 teaspoon sea salt

Frosting

4½ tablespoons arrowroot rocks or kuzu

6 tablespoons rice milk or almond milk

6 tablespoons agar flakes

350 ml/12 fl oz/1½ cups water

60 g/2 oz/½ cup cocoa powder

800 ml/28 fl oz/2½ cups maple syrup

1½ teaspoons vanilla extract

½ teaspoon sea salt

Preheat the oven to 180°C/350°F/gas mark 4. Lightly oil and flour two 23 cm/9 inch springform cake tins. Sift together the flours, baking powder, bicarbonate of soda, cocoa, cinnamon, xanthan gum and salt in a medium mixing bowl. In a second mixing bowl, whisk together the oil, maple syrup, vinegar, vanilla and water until smooth. With a wooden spoon, stir the wet and dry ingredients together. Try not over-mix.

Divide the batter equally between the two prepared cake tins and bake on the middle rack of the preheated oven for 35 minutes or until a skewer inserted into the centre comes out clean. Do not open the oven door for the first 30 minutes, as the cake may fall flat. Cool completely before removing and decorating.

Make the frosting by dissolving the arrowroot or kuzu in the rice milk; set aside. Place the agar flakes and water in a small saucepan over a medium heat. Simmer and stir occasionally until the agar is dissolved, about 5 minutes. Whisk in the cocoa powder, maple syrup, sea salt and vanilla extract. Add to the agar mixture, raise the heat to medium, and cook for another minute. Pour the frosting into a container and refrigerate for about 30–45 minutes until firm. Purée in a food processor until creamy before spreading on the cake.

Chocolate and Mango Tart

The combination of mango with chocolate is truly unique. This a dense tart that is best served thinly sliced, as it's quite rich and decadent. If you like, you can replace the mangoes with other fruits such as sautéed pears or figs, or fresh raspberries macerated with raspberry Stolli (vodka), sprinkled in just before baking. Served cold with Crème Anglaise (page 147), fresh fruits, or hot out of the oven with a scoop of mango ice cream. Yum!

SERVES 6–8

1 x recipe Basic tart Dough (page 65)

Sautéed mangoes

2 firm but ripe mangoes, chopped into 1 cm/½ inch cubes

3 tablespoons unrefined golden caster (superfine) sugar

2 tablespoons margarine or ghee or coconut butter

Filling

115 g/4 oz/½ cup margarine or ghee or coconut butter

150 g/5 oz/1 cup bittersweet chocolate, e.g. Valrhona 61% cocoa solids, finely chopped

1 organic egg

3 organic egg yolks

2½ tablespoons unrefined golden caster (superfine) sugar

½ teaspoon vanilla extract

pinch of sea salt (optional)

Prepare the mangoes by tossing them all in the sugar. Take a frying pan and melt the margarine or ghee or coconut butter over a high heat. Once hot and bubbly, add the cubed mangoes. You need to almost sear them on a high heat so that they are caramelized but are still firm and keep their shape. Stir the mangoes around a bit, take off the heat and immediately place on a large plate so that they cool to room temperature.

To make the filling, preheat the oven to 190°C/375°F/gas mark 5. Melt the margarine or ghee or coconut butter with the chocolate in a bowl over simmering water or in a microwave, till liquid but not hot. In a separate bowl, mix the egg, yolks, sugar, vanilla extract and salt (if using) together so that they are just incorporated, not whisked.

Take a rubber spatula and blend the chocolate and fats together once more as they have probably separated during melting. Do this step without beating air into them, just as you would with Dark Chocolate Ganache (page 144). Make sure the chocolate and butter mixture is barely warm and not hot before slowly adding the egg mixture and gently blend until just smooth.

Scatter the mangoes evenly over the base of the pastry case, pour the chocolate filling over, and bake in the preheated oven for about 15–20 minutes. The tart is ready when the sides start to set. Don't be tempted to cook it for longer as the tart will set as it cools. Best served hot or cold.

Gateau aux Noix (Walnut Cake)

This is a simple cake that can be eaten for afternoon tea or dressed up with Vanilla Buttercream and served as a dessert. It's super-light and incredibly moist but with the heady aroma of toasted walnuts coming through. I like pairing it with a sweet dessert wine, but a cup of hot tea will do very well!

SERVES 6–8

8 organic eggs, separated

250 g/9 oz/1¼ cups unrefined icing (confectioners') sugar

1 vanilla pod

60 g/2½ oz/¼ cup gluten-free breadcrumbs, semi-dried

juice of 1 lemon

250 g/9 oz/2½ cups ground walnuts

60 g/2 oz/¼ cup ghee or coconut butter or margarine, melted and cooled

1 tablespoon walnut oil

8 walnut pieces

Preheat the oven to 180°C/350°F/gas mark 4. Line a 23 cm/9 inch baking tin with lightly greased and floured parchment paper and set aside.

Whisk the egg yolks with 200 g/7 oz/1¾ cups of the icing sugar until pale and creamy and at ribbon stage. Split the vanilla pod lengthways, scrape out the seeds with the back of a knife and add to the mixture.

Blend the breadcrumbs with the lemon juice and ground walnuts using a wooden spoon. Whisk the rest of the sugar with the egg whites until stiff and glossy. Fold the egg yolk mixture into the egg whites, followed by the breadcrumb mixture.

Mix the melted ghee or coconut butter or margarine together with the walnut oil and then fold into the mixture. Try not to over-mix, or the mixture will lose volume. Pour into the prepared tin and bake in the preheated oven for about 40–45 minutes or until a skewer inserted into the cake comes out clean.

Leave to cool in the tin. Once cool turn on to a wire rack and remove the parchment paper. This cake is best served with Luscious Lemon Cream (page 152) or Vanilla Buttercream (page 155).

Moorish Orange Cake with Sweet Saffron Glaze

'Naranja' in Spanish comes from the Persian word for oranges, and this cake was brought over from that part of the world by the Moors. I've added a saffron glaze not only for its sumptuous colour but also because it seems to go quite well with the oranges and ground almonds and is widely used in Persian sweetmeats. Serve the cake sliced thinly as an after-dinner dessert or generously for afternoon tea.

SERVES 8–10

Cake

1 orange

250 g/9 oz/1½ cups ground almonds

½ teaspoon baking powder

¼ teaspoon sea salt

3 organic eggs

225 g/8 oz/1 cup unrefined golden caster (superfine) sugar

1 teaspoon vanilla extract

Glaze

2 tablespoons hot water

1 teaspoon orange-flower water

4–5 saffron threads

125 g/4 oz/1 cup unrefined icing (confectioners') sugar

Make the cake by putting the orange into a pan and add water to cover. Bring to the boil, then reduce to a simmer, cover the pan and cook for about 1 hour or until the orange is soft. Strain, and let it cool to room temperature. (You can also cook it for about a minute or two in the microwave.) Cut the orange in half and remove the pips. Place the two halves in a food processor and whizz until you have a lovely smooth paste.

Preheat your oven to 180°C/350°F/gas mark 4. Grease a 20 cm/8 inch springform tin, line it with baking parchment, grease and flour it and set it aside.

Sift the ground almonds, baking powder and sea salt. Whisk the eggs, sugar and vanilla extract until thick and pale and at ribbon stage. Fold in the orange purée and then the almond mixture. Pour the mixture into the prepared tin and bake in the preheated oven for about 40–50 minutes or until a skewer inserted in the middle comes out clean. Resist flipping it out and let it cool completely in the tin.

Make the glaze by heating the water, orange-flower water and saffron until very hot. Whisk in the icing sugar a little at a time until the mixture coats the back of a spoon and is free from any lumps. Pour over the cake and let it set.

Dacquoise

This recipe was given to me by my teacher Laurent Duchene, who is a Meilleur Ouvrier de France (MOF) and is now the owner of one of the best pastry shops in Paris. I have spent time in his kitchen, which is mostly, and surprisingly, run by talented and energetic young women. Chef Laurent uses the best ingredients available – butter from Charente, Callebaut chocolate, the best fruits and plump Madagascar vanilla. It's a true labour of love!

Dacquoise is very similar to a meringue, but since it contains ground almonds it's heartier and therefore sturdier. It belongs to the family of macarons. It's a versatile base that's great for layering in different mousses, fruit and ice cream cakes.

SERVES 6–8

8 organic egg whites

pinch of sea salt

200 g/7 oz/1 cup unrefined golden caster (superfine) sugar, mixed with 2 teaspoons vanilla sugar

150 g/5 oz/1¼ cups ground almonds or hazelnuts

85 g/3 oz/½ cup skinned almonds or hazelnuts, very finely chopped and ground

For this recipe, you can prepare your baking tray in one of two ways: either use baking parchment and draw 2 x 20 cm/8 inch circles with a pencil, then flip the paper over (you will still be able to see the drawings), or use 2 lightly oiled 20 cm/8 inch flan moulds or rings lined with baking parchment. Either way, prepare 2 pastry bags fitted with a plain medium nozzle.

Preheat the oven to 180°C/350°F/gas mark 4. Using a KitchenAid (or other food mixer) fitted with a whisk attachment, whisk the egg whites and salt until foamy. Add the sugar in three stages, whisking until you have stiff peaks. Stop the machine and quickly fold in the ground almonds. Divide the mixture in half and spoon into the pastry bags. Starting in the middle of each circle and moving outwards, pipe the mixture until you reach the edge of the pencil line or flan ring. Bake in the preheated oven for about 20 minutes or until puffed up and pale gold in colour.

Allow to cool before adding Vanilla Buttercream (page 155) or Crème Mousseline (page 146) and top with raspberries, lychees or any other fruit you fancy. You can even layer the Dacquoise with ice cream! Sprinkle with icing (confectioners') sugar and decorate.

Un-cheesecake

I used to love eating cheesecake. Tucking into a thick creamy slice topped with macerated berries was one of the best pleasures in life, no matter what the calorie count. But what happens when you love cheesecake and you can't eat it any more? You also can't eat soya, so out of the window goes the soya cream cheese alternative. I once watched someone eat a cheesecake and I almost broke down in tears. This recipe isn't like New York-style cheesecakes, more cake-like and chunky, but nonetheless creamy and dense with the right crust, and topped with delicious fresh fruits.

SERVES 6-8

2 tablespoons kuzu or 4 tablespoons arrowroot

335 ml/12 fl oz/1½ cups rice milk or almond milk

1 vanilla pod

350 ml/12 fl oz/1½ cups coconut milk

225 g/8 oz/1 cup light brown sugar

2½ teaspoons agar agar powder or 3 tablespoons agar agar flakes

3 tablespoons fresh lemon juice and zest, finely chopped

2 organic eggs + 2 extra yolks, lightly whisked

Shell

160 g/5½ oz/1½ cups gluten-free cream cracker crumbs

4 tablespoons margarine, ghee or coconut butter, melted and cooled

2 teaspoons lemon zest, finely chopped

Preheat the oven to 160°C/325°F/gas mark 3. Make the shell by mixing the cream cracker crumbs with the margarine, ghee or coconut butter and lemon zest in a bowl or plastic ziplock bag. Spread in a 23 cm/9 inch spring-form flan tin and press down with your fingers, making sure you do this evenly without missing the sides. Bake for 10–15 minutes only. Leave to cool.

Strain the cashews and whizz in a food processor until creamy fluffy and smooth. Stop the machine from time to time to let it rest as it may take 2–3 minutes to get a smooth enough cream.

Meanwhile, add the kuzu or arrowroot to 115 ml/4 fl oz/½ cup of the rice or almond milk and set aside. Split the vanilla pod in half and scrape out its seeds with the back of a knife. Put it into a heavy pan with the coconut milk, the rest of the rice or almond milk, the sugar, agar agar, lemon juice and zest. Bring to the boil, then lower the temperature and boil for 1–2 minutes if using agar agar powder or 4–5 minutes using agar agar flakes, continuously stirring, until the mixture starts to thicken. Add the kuzu or arrowroot mixture and stir until it comes to the boil again – it will thicken considerably. If using arrowroot, take it off the heat now. If using kuzu, let it boil for 1–2 minutes more. Then fold in the cashew cream.

Let the mixture cool completely before whisking in the egg mixture, then pour it into the prepared shell. Bake in the preheated oven for 45–60 minutes or until risen and lightly golden.

Leave in the tin and refrigerate for at least 4 hours or overnight. To remove from the tin, run a knife around the edge of the cheesecake to loosen. Top with berries, peaches or any other fruit of your choice. Yummy.

No-bake Carrot Cake ♡

So you want all the flavour of a carrot cake but don't feel like cooking it? You can have it in this easy-to-make yummy, healthy and unusual version. The first time I came across a raw cake I was deeply skeptical. But once I had taken a bite, I was hooked. Since then, I've not been able to stop eating raw desserts. This cake is hearty and light at the same time. The combination of the fresh carrots and the nutty frosting is simply divine. You'll become addicted to it and find yourself craving it!

SERVES 6–8

800 g/1¾ lbs/5½ cups grated carrots

175 g/6 oz/1½ cups walnuts, finely chopped

45 g/1½ oz/½ cup desiccated coconut

150 g/5 oz dried papaya or mangoes, roughly chopped

2 tablespoons finely chopped orange zest

215 g/7½ oz/1½ cups dried dates, pitted and chopped

juice of 1 large orange (organic)

1 teaspoon vanilla extract

2 tablespoons ground flax seeds

85 ml/3 fl oz/⅓ cup agave nectar

1 teaspoon ground cinnamon

pinch of sea salt

grated coconut and grated nutmeg, to decorate

Cashew Nut Purée Frosting

175 g/6 oz/1½ cups raw cashews, or any other raw untreated nut

3 tablespoons agave nectar

85 ml/3 fl oz/⅓ cup fresh orange juice

½ teaspoon vanilla extract

Take a 20 cm/8 inch cake tin or loaf tin and line it with clingfilm, leaving a little extra hanging over the edge.

1) Mix the carrots, walnuts, coconut, papaya or mangoes and orange zest in a large bowl. 2) Place the dates, orange juice, vanilla extract, flax seeds, agave nectar, cinnamon and salt in a food processor. Turn the machine on and blend until the mixture becomes soft. Stop the machine and scrape down the sides if you need to until you get a nice smooth purée. 3) Mix the purée with the carrot mixture. You may need to use your hands, so go ahead and mix it all up until it clings together. Place the mixture in the prepared tin and spread it around, using your hands, until smooth and level. Cover with more clingfilm and leave it in the refrigerator overnight.

4) Make the frosting by placing the cashews in enough water to cover them and let them soak for about 2 hours. 5) Drain off the water and place the nuts in a food processor or blender with the agave nectar, orange juice and vanilla extract. Add more sweetness if you need to. Blend the mixture until creamy and smooth.

6) Take the carrot cake out of the refrigerator and flip it over on to a serving dish. Remove the clingfilm and shape it a little with your hands if necessary. 7) Frost with the cashew nut purée, decorate with grated coconut and grated nutmeg and serve.

Old-fashioned Carrot Cake ♡

This cake is good on its own or with a light Vanilla Buttercream (page 155). As with other cakes, cut slices as you need them so that they retain their moisture. You can add walnuts, almonds or pinenuts to the mixture to make it super chunky.

SERVES 6–8

200 g/7 oz/1½ cups gluten-free flour

90 g/3 oz/⅓ cup sweet rice flour (Mochiko)

½ teaspoon bicarbonate of soda (baking soda)

1½ teaspoons baking powder

1 teaspoon xanthan gum

2 teaspoons cinnamon

pinch of sea salt

115 ml/4 fl oz/½ cup light olive oil or safflower oil

115 g/4 oz/½ cup margarine or ghee or coconut butter, at room temperature

250 g/9 oz/1½ cups unrefined light brown sugar

4 organic eggs

1 teaspoon vanilla extract

90 g/3 oz/⅓ cup apple purée

70 g/2½ oz/½ cup chopped dried dates or whole raisins

400 g/14 oz/3 cups finely grated carrots

Preheat the oven to 180°C/350°F/gas mark 4. Prepare a 20 cm/8 inch round cake tin by lightly oiling the inside and lining the bottom with baking parchment. Sift the flours, bicarbonate of soda, baking powder, xanthan gum, cinnamon and salt together and set aside.

In a KitchenAid (or other food mixer) fitted with a paddle attachment, mix the oil and the margarine or ghee. Add the sugar, eggs, vanilla extract and apple purée. Blend well. Add the dates or raisins, and the grated carrots.

Now add the flour mixture and mix, using a wooden spoon, until just blended. Pour the mixture into the prepared tin and bake in the preheated oven for about 30–40 minutes or until a skewer inserted into the centre comes out clean. Turn on to a wire rack to cool.

This cake is best served with Vanilla Buttercream. Cool completely before spreading on top.

Strawberry Frangipane Tart

In the sixteenth century, an Italian nobleman called Marquis Muzio Frangipani created a perfume for scenting gloves based on bitter almonds. It was so popular in Paris that bakers and patissiers called this tart frangipane, to take advantage of the scent's popularity. You can make one single tart or make mini-tartlets to serve as petits fours. The freshness of the strawberries marries well with the almond frangipane and rum.

SERVES 6–8

115 g/4 oz/½ cup margarine or ghee or coconut butter

zest of ½ lemon, finely chopped

115 g/4 oz/1 cup unrefined golden caster (superfine) sugar

2 organic eggs, lightly whisked

4 teaspoons rum

1 teaspoon vanilla extract

2 tablespoons gluten-free flour

85 g/3 oz/¾ cup ground almonds

50 g/2 oz/½ cup almond nibs

300 g/10 oz organic strawberries

175 g/6 oz/½ cup apricot jam

1 x recipe Basic Tart Dough (page 65), baked blind for 10 minutes only

Preheat the oven to 180°C/350°F/gas mark 4. Cream the margarine or ghee, the zest and sugar in a KitchenAid (or other food mixer) until pale and creamy. Add the eggs, rum and vanilla extract and mix a little more.

Add the flour, then the ground almonds and finally the almond nibs. Pour this mixture into your prepared pastry case, even out the top with a spoon or spatula, and bake in the preheated oven for about 25–30 minutes or until golden. The mix will fill the tart part way leaving enough room for the strawberry topping.

Meanwhile, slice the strawberries in half. Prepare a glaze by mixing the apricot jam with 1–2 tablespoons of filtered water. Heat until boiling and leave to cool slightly.

Once the tart is baked and cooled, arrange the strawberries all over the top and glaze them quickly with the apricot glaze – the French call this 'nappage'. The strawberries need to be glazed all over so that they shine and look fresh, but be careful not to use too much glaze. Cut and serve.

4

feather light

From mousses and puddings, to flans and truffles, these light desserts are a mixture of revisited classics and **innovative** sweets. **Create** creaminess by adding non-dairy milks to truffles and rice puddings. Give them texture and **depth** with the new-age gelatines. **Lighten** with whipped coconut cream and air. Fold in fresh fruit purées for a tangy taste. Add **crunch** with nuts and sesame seeds. Most are **quick** to prepare and some are easy to freeze and bake or assemble at the last minute. Have them handy. They go down a **treat** after a meal but are also fabulous for afternoon tea or just as a sweet **nibble**.

Tropical Fruit Mousse

Once I discovered that coconut cream could be whipped, all the possibilities came rushing in! Especially this beautiful dessert, which is light and fruity with just the right amount of sweetness. If you are unable to find coconut cream, simply take a can of coconut milk and refrigerate for an hour or more. Skim off the hard cream that will have come to the surface leaving the liquid behind. You may need up to 3 cans for this recipe. Find a nice mould to make the mousse in so that it sets well and comes out in a clean shape. It helps to have the ingredients around the same temperature, so that you get a fluffy mousse without any lumps.

SERVES 6

1 x Sponge Cake (page 65)

Tropical Fruit Mousse

3 gelatine leaves or 1 packet powdered gelatine

350 ml/12 fl oz/1½ cups coconut cream, cold

200 ml/7 fl oz/1 cup tropical fruit purée, such as passionfruit, mango, pineapple

2 tablespoons unrefined golden caster (superfne) sugar

70 ml/2½ fl oz/⅓ cup Simple Syrup (page 158)

200 g/7 oz/1 cup chopped tropical fruits, such as pineapple or mango

Tropical Punch Syrup

300 ml/10 fl oz/1⅓ cups Simple Syrup (page 158)

100 ml/3½ fl oz/½ cup Malibu or light rum

Prepare your 15 cm/6 inch mould or line a bowl with cling film and set aside. Cut the sponge cake into 3 thin layers and set aside 2 of them. Keep the third layer for another dessert.

Soak the gelatine in cold water until it becomes soft.

Meanwhile, whip the coconut cream until fluffy and stiff. Put a quarter of the fruit purée into a small pan with the sugar and the sugar syrup. Add the strained gelatine leaves or powder mixed with water. Heat this mixture over a medium heat for about 30–40 seconds, until the gelatine has completely dissolved. Try not to let it come to the boil or it will lose some of its setting properties.

Now this part is important, but very easy to do. Add the rest of the fruit purée to the gelatine mixture. The whole thing is now at about room temperature, so it's ready to be folded into the whipped coconut cream. Add a little of the whipped coconut cream to the fruit mixture and whisk. Now add the rest in one go. Still using your whisk but using folding motions, stir just until there are no visible white lumps. Pour half the mixture into your mould and cover with a layer of sponge cake.

Make the tropical punch syrup by mixing together the simple syrup and Malibu or rum. Generously soak the cake with some of the tropical punch syrup using a pastry brush, cover with a layer of half the chopped fruits and pour on the remaining mousse.

Cover with another layer of fruit, and repeat with a layer of sponge.

Soak well with the remaining tropical punch syrup, cover, and chill in the refrigerator for at least 4 hours. Flip on to a serving plate and decorate with tropical fruits of your choice.

Heavenly Grass

Kanten, or agar agar, is an ancient natural gelatine made from a bright sea vegetable, a form of algae, that has almost no flavour and zero calories. It's known as heavenly grass in Japanese. It sets very quickly at room temperature and stays that way even if you leave it out of the refrigerator, although refrigeration is recommended.

You can use any fruit you like as long as it's not very acidic. Kiwis, pineapples and strawberries tend to combat the gelling agent in agar agar and give you softer gelatine. If you like your desserts a little more firm, cooking these fruits for 5 minutes will destroy those enzymes that combat the setting process.

HONEYDEW MELON AND POMEGRANATE KANTEN

450 ml/16 fl oz/2 cups unsweetened apple juice or white grape juice

1 teaspoon agar agar powder

1 tablespoon unrefined golden caster (superfine) sugar

½ honeydew melon, cut into 1 cm/½ inch squares or made into miniature balls using a melon baller

seeds of ½ pomegranate

2 teaspoon kuzu (optional, see below)

In a saucepan, bring the apple juice to the boil with the agar agar and sugar. Reduce the heat and simmer for about 5 minutes, stirring frequently. Meanwhile, prepare 4 clear glasses. Pour the hot liquid into the glasses and leave to cool for about 10 minutes before adding the melon and pomegranate seeds. Leave to set in the refrigerator for 1 hour or more before serving.

Variations

You can replace the melon with peaches, plums, apples or anything other fruit you fancy. I like to top this with whipped cream, lightly toasted nuts and a drizzle of Fruit Coulis (page 143).

For a more custard-style kanten, dissolve 2 teaspoons of kuzu in a little water and add to the hot fruit juice just before you are about to take it off the heat. Allow this version to rest overnight before serving.

YOKAN

You can also use agar agar to make traditional Japanese wagashis – an edible art form inspired by nature and the four seasons. These confectioneries are amazingly beautiful and modern-looking but date back as far as AD 600! The recipe below is a simple form of wagashi using agar agar as a base, a Japanese form of Turkish delight but better. They are best accompanied by green tea.

685 ml/1¼ pints/3 cups filtered water

1½ teaspoons agar agar powder

425 g/15 oz/2 cups puréed sweetened adzuki beans, or chestnut purée, store-bought or home-made

pinch of sea salt

Bring the water and agar agar to the boil and simmer gently for about 3 minutes, stirring frequently. Add the bean or chestnut purée and salt, and stir for another 2–3 minutes. Pour into a 20 cm/8 inch cake tin or tray and put into the refrigerator until it sets firm. Cut into squares and serve.

Chocolate Fondue

The word fondue comes from the French word 'fondre', which means to melt. Although cheese fondues date back to the eighteenth century, dessert fondues were only created in the 1960s and became very popular in the '70s. It's a great way to end a romantic meal for two. It's also an easy and fun option when you're catering for a large party. It gives everyone an excuse to interact. Chop any fruits you have handy. Cut up store-bought gluten-free cakes or shortbreads, even left-over ones you've made earlier. Place all your dippables on a pretty tray and decorate with whole fruits or even just one fresh exotic flower – then get dipping! Fondues are great crowd-pleasers.

SERVES 4

85 ml/3 fl oz/⅓ cup coconut milk

200 g/7 oz milk (semisweet) chocolate, such as Gianduja, finely chopped

tiny pinch of sea salt (optional)

You will also need a fondue pot

Heat the coconut milk until almost boiling and pour over the chocolate. Add the salt (if using) and stir until smooth, and pour into a fondue pot. Serve immediately.

Variations

You can vary the flavours by adding ½ teaspoon of finely chopped orange zest to the coconut milk. Pour over the chocolate, then add 1 tablespoon of Cointreau or Grand Marnier.

You can also heat up a Fruit Coulis (page 143) on its own in the fondue pot instead of chocolate for a fresher taste.

You can always use a clean new oil burner if you don't have a fondue pot – it does the same thing!

Thai Beignets

The first time I had these lovely bananas was in Thailand, on the island of Koh Samui. We met a very interesting Mick Jagger-type character who had made his fortune and had decided to open a restaurant overlooking a small group of beautiful islands jutting out from the turquoise sea. The beignets came piping hot and were served with cool and fragrant coconut ice cream. They were different from the beignets I'd had in the past. They were still crusty on the outside but once you bit into them they had the consistency of cake, filled with crunchy sesame seeds. The combination of the two coupled with the evening ocean breeze was unforgettable.

SERVES 6

10 small Asian bananas or 5 regular ones

1.1 litres/2 pints/5 cups high oleic safflower oil or sunflower oil

85 g/3 oz/¾ cup rice flour

30 g/1 oz/¼ cup tapioca flour

3 tablespoons unrefined golden caster (superfine) sugar

35 g/1¼ oz/¼ cup sesame seeds, lightly toasted

½ teaspoon sea salt

85 g/3 oz/¾ cup unsweetend coconut powder

1 teaspoon baking powder

115 ml/¼ pt/½ cup coconut milk

225 ml/8 fl oz/1 cup water

Peel the bananas and cut lengthwise into 3 or 4 pieces. Heat the oil in a deep-fryer or deep pan to about 190°C/375°F. In a medium bowl, whisk together the rice flour, tapioca flour, sugar, sesame seeds, salt, coconut powder and baking powder. Mix the coconut milk and water together and slowly add to the dry mixture in stages. You'll end up with a nice thick batter.

Dip the banana slices in the batter and lower them carefully into the hot oil a few at a time. Remove them once they have turned golden and drain on kitchen paper. You can serve them on their own or with some cool Lemongrass and Coconut Sorbet (page 118).

Chocolate Pot au Crème

This pot au crème recipe is made on the stove, so it eliminates the whole steaming method and the possibility of curdling in the oven. Its creamy texture is somewhere between a mousse au chocolat and a pudding, but richer. I prefer to use a chocolate that's a bit smoother and not as strong as those that are 70% cocoa solids and over.

SERVES 6-8

250 g/9 oz dark (bittersweet) chocolate (minimum 65% cocoa solids), finely chopped

2 gelatine leaves or 1 teaspoon agar agar

Crème Anglaise

1 large vanilla pod

500 ml/17 fl oz/2 cups rice milk or almond milk

50 g/2 oz/¼ cup unrefined golden caster (superfine) sugar

5 organic egg yolks, lightly whisked

45 g/1½ oz/¼ cup Vance's DariFree milk powder

2 tablespoons grapeseed oil or ghee

pinch of sea salt (optional)

Follow the directions for making Crème Anglaise on page 147.

Once the crème is ready, blend in the agar agar and allow it to cook for about 2–3 minutes, stirring frequently. If you are using gelatine leaves, take the créme anglaise off the heat, add the gelatine and stir until dissolved.

Then stir in the chopped chocolate gently to melt all the chocolate pieces. Immediately pour the custard into individual pot de crème dishes, flan moulds or serving cups. Cover with clingfilm, allowing it to touch the surface of the crème so that no skin forms later on, just like the Crème Patissèrie recipe on page 146. Leave to cool. Let the pots chill in the refrigerator for at least 3 hours or more before serving.

You can top them with coconut Crème Chantilly (page 148), Fruit Coulis (page 143) or just eat them on their own with a side order of Pistachio and Raspberry Financiers (page 57) or Crispy Coconut Tuiles (page 104).

Grandma's Rice Pudding

I was blessed with the loveliest grandmother in the world. She used to make these whenever we went to visit her, and she'd have them lined up in pretty little bowls in the refrigerator, nice and cold, to be drizzled with some caramel-like grape molasses. This is a whole different take on the usual rice pudding.

SERVES 6–8

115 g/4 oz/½ cup arborio or basmati rice

675 g/1¼ pts/3 cups almond milk or rice milk

½ vanilla pod

tiniest pinch of sea salt

½ teaspoon ground cardamom (optional)

Place the rice in a saucepan, cover with water and bring to the boil. Allow to cook for 15 minutes or until al dente. To check it's ready, take a rice kernel and squeeze it between your fingers – it should be soft but still have a hard centre.

Add the rice milk, vanilla pod and salt and bring the mixture to the boil again. Reduce the heat to low and cook, stirring from time to time, until the liquid evaporates and the rice grains are nicely coated with the creamy milk. This will take about 20–30 minutes. Add the cardamom (if using) and cook for another 10 minutes, but this time stir frequently to make sure the rice doesn't catch at the bottom. Pour the pudding into a heatproof serving dish or individual bowls.

Cool to room temperature, then chill in the refrigerator. Best served very cold, with a drizzle of grape molasses, maple syrup, honey or even some lovely sour cherry jam.

Chocolate Chestnut Truffles

These truffles are incredibly simple to make. The inside of the truffles, or ganache as the French call it, is made with rice or almond milk instead of double (heavy) cream, which makes it lower in fat. You can also use coconut cream for richer centres. The result is a creamy-rich combination of dark chocolate with the nutty earthy taste of chestnuts and a hint of kirsch. There are endless flavours you can pair dark chocolate with, such as ginger, pistachio, raspberry, bitter orange, passion fruit and even honey and lavender.

MAKES 36 SMALL TRUFFLES

450 g/1 lb dark (bittersweet) chocolate (minimum 70% cocoa solids), finely chopped

175 ml/6 fl oz/¾ cup coconut cream or rice milk or almond milk

130 g/4½ oz ⅔ cup chestnut purée flavoured with vanilla (crème de marrons)

4 tablespoons margarine or ghee or coconut butter, at room temperature

225 g/8 oz/2 cups cocoa powder

130 g/4½ oz/scant 1 cup chocolate couverture, finely chopped

1 teaspoon kirsch (optional)

Place the dark chocolate in a bowl. Heat the rice or almond milk until very hot but not boiling, pour over the chocolate and keep stirring until smooth. Blend in the chestnut purée and add the margarine or ghee or coconut butter in small pieces, letting each piece blend thoroughly before you add any more. This is your ganache – cover with clingfilm and put in the refrigerator until set.

Line a small baking tray with baking parchment, sprinkle with most of the cocoa powder and set aside. Put the chocolate couverture in the microwave until almost melted, then remove, stir, and set aside on a small towel (this is so that the chocolate doesn't come into contact with the cold work surface and solidify). The chocolate will continue to melt after it comes out of the microwave. When it has completely melted, stir in the kirsch if using.

Using either a mini scoop, a melon baller or a teaspoon, scoop out pieces of ganache and quickly roll into evenly-sized balls. To prevent the ganache from melting and sticking to your fingers, lightly sprinkle your hands with cocoa powder, icing (confectioners') sugar or cornflour (corn starch). Dip the balls in the melted chocolate and immediately roll them in cocoa powder on one side. Wait 3–4 seconds then flip the truffles onto the other side and roll in cocoa powder to finish. Allow them to harden before serving.

Crispy Coconut Tuiles ♡

The delicate and crispy texture of these tuiles (meaning lace in French), marries very well with ice cream, sorbet or a fresh fruit salad. They can be baked in advance and stored in an airtight container, and the mixture can be frozen for up to 1 month. The mixture needs to be made in advance and allowed to rest in the refrigerator overnight.

MAKES 48

2 teaspoons margarine or ghee or coconut butter

350 g/10 oz/1½ cups unrefined golden caster (superfine) sugar

30 g/1 oz/¼ cup gluten-free flour

175 g/6 oz/2 cups desiccated coconut

¼ teaspoon xanthan gum

4 organic eggs

dash of sea salt

Using a KitchenAid (or other food mixer) fitted with a paddle attachment, mix the margarine or ghee and the sugar together for about 3 minutes. The mixture will not be creamy and fluffy. Sift the flour with the salt, desiccated coconut and xanthan gum and set aside.

With the machine running on medium low, add the eggs in 3 or 4 stages, stopping the machine to scrape down the sides if you need to. Once you've poured all the eggs into the butter and sugar mixture, fold in the flour mixture until just incorporated. Transfer the mixture to a bowl, cover with clingfilm and refrigerate overnight.

Preheat the oven to 150°C/300°F/gas mark 2. Line a baking tray with baking parchment or a silicon liner. Now you need to create a template, for which you will need a large plastic lid from an ice cream or yogurt container. Using a scalpel, razor blade or sharp knife, carefully cut out an 8 cm/3 inch diameter circle from the centre without cutting the outside rim.

Place the template on the prepared tray and spoon ½ teaspoon of the cold dough on top. Spread the dough until you get an even film, then remove the template, scraping any dough remaining on the spatula and template back into the bowl. Continue until the tray is filled, leaving a 5–8 cm/2–3 inch space between the tuiles. Put the tray back into the refrigerator for about 10 minutes, then transfer to the preheated oven. (You need to make sure the mixture is cold before it goes into the oven, as this will help the tuiles not to spread too much.)

Bake in the preheated oven for about 12–15 minutes, rotating the tray halfway into the cooking time to ensure even baking. The tuiles will be golden.

The final little trick is to remove the tuiles from the baking sheet as soon as they come out of the oven so that they don't get stuck to the lining. If you'd like to be adventurous, lift the hot tuiles, place them round a rolling pin, and leave to cool completely before removing.

Fresh Konnyaku Summer Rolls ♡

What if you were told that there exists a vegetable that is high in dietary fibre, rich in minerals, cleanses your digestive system, suppresses the appetite, is tasteless and virtually calorie and fat-free? How about if it also reduces cholesterol, controls blood sugar levels in diabetics and is perfect as a fat replacer in certain products? Would you think it's too good to be true? Well, konnyaku, or devil's tongue as some call it, has been consumed by the Japanese for nearly 1,500 years for just those reasons. This tubular root vegetable is broken down into a gelatinous powder and used mainly as a thickening agent, but is also transformed into capsules, glass noodles or chunks like tofu. It is the Japanese woman's secret for staying slim, as it has the power to make you feel full. I think that we're going to see a lot more of this miraculous vegetable in the years to come.

Here I wanted to come up with a dessert that I can eat without feeling too guilty, as it is extremely low in fat and calories. I think this is one of the best ways to enjoy konnyaku, as it has a rather tough gelatinous texture. By chopping it finely with some crunchy apples, you won't even know it's there. Use any fruit combination you like. Just make sure the fruits are very fresh and firm.

SERVES 4

100 g/3½ oz/½ cup konnyaku noodles or chunks

1 large green apple

5–6 lychees, sliced

5–6 strawberries, hulled and sliced thinly

2–3 red plums, pitted and sliced thinly

2–3 tablespoons saké (optional)

4 rice paper wrappers

12–15 mint leaves

115 ml/4 fl oz/½ cup fresh orange juice, mango juice, passion fruit juice or pineapple juice

agave nectar, to taste

Blanch the konnyaku briefly in boiling water for about 10–20 seconds only. Drain and wash with cold water. Dice the konnyaku noodles or chunks and the green apple. Mix all the fruits up in a bowl with the saké (if using) and put the bowl in the refrigerator for a few minutes.

Take another larger bowl and soak the rice paper wrappers in some water until soft. Dab the excess water away with kitchen paper and place them on a board. Add two or three mint leaves to each wrapper and place some fruits in the middle of each one. Turn the sides over to stop the fruits falling out (like proper spring rolls), and roll them up. Cover tightly with clingfilm and leave in the refrigerator while you prepare the dipping sauce.

Finely chop the remaining mint and mix it with the fruit juice and a little agave nectar, to taste. You can also serve these spring rolls with Fruit Coulis (page 143) or even Nut Anglaise (page 151).

Unwrap the rolls and dip away!

Espumas

Espumas in Spanish means foams. This aerated foam can be created using a little gadget by the name of Profi Whip or Gormet Whip, made by ISI. By simply pouring the measured ingredients and adding a mini gas canister, you can create all sorts of light and airy mousses. One of the most talented chefs and inventors, Ferrán Adriá, the chef at the renowned El Bulli restaurant near Barcelona, took this concept to new heights by creating unusual sweet and savoury textured mousses. For a dairy intolerant person like myself, this little tool opened the door to all sorts of new possibilities. You can create 'glass desserts' by layering clear shot glasses or martini glasses with cake, nuts, coulis, mousses and gelees.

Although general instructions are given in the manual, here are several important points you'll want to remember before attempting the following recipes:

- Always strain the purées or sauces so that nothing can clog up the machine.
- The container needs to be 80–90% full whatever the size of your whipping machine. Less than that will result in a limp mousse.
- You will need to get of rid of anything that is in the machine before opening it. That means piping everything out in order to empty it.
- Try and not use more than two gas canisters (depending on the size of the machine), as the finished product may fall flat after it has been piped.

Three easy steps:

- Fill the container with the liquid with or without gelatine.
- Close the lid and empty 1 or 2 gas canisters according to the instructions and size of the machine (1 or ½ litre)
- Shake the Profi Whip or Gourmet Whip 3–4 times and place in the refrigerator for at least 30 minutes before using.

FRUIT MOUSSES

Any fruit puree or juice will produce very good results. Fruit purees can be used alone, but fruit juices need some bulking up with gelatine. Pipe over fresh fruits or other desserts for a fruity lightness.

750 g/1½ lbs fresh raspberries/strawberries/mango

200 ml/7 fl oz Simple Syrup (page 158)

200 ml/7 fl oz filtered water

2 gelatine leaves, softened in water and the excess squeezed out

In a food processor, blend the fruits, syrup and water until smooth. Strain out the seeds or pulp. Heat ½ cup of the fruit mixture and 2 'bloomed' gelatine leaves over the stove. Pour back with the rest of the fruit puree and place in the machine. Follow the steps above and use.

VANILLA MOUSSE

This is an unbelievably light creamy mousse that you can top fruits, trifles, sundaes and tarts with. Follow the Crème Anglaise recipe on page 147. Cool and pour into the machine. Follow instructions and cool in the refrigerator for at least 30 minutes.

Sweet Pumpkin Flan ♡

The thing you'll probably miss most when you discover you are dairy-intolerant is the mouth-feel you get from cream-laden desserts. This recipe says: no longer! This flan has all the creaminess without the actual cream, and it's also very low in fat, though you'd never guess. It's sumptuous, silky, with a bite from the pumpkin and a hit from fragrant cinnamon, nutmeg and allspice. Serve it with a dollop of sweetened Mock Whipped Cream (page 148) and a drizzle of Dulce de Leche (page 142) and you'll keep asking for more.

SERVES 6

115 g/4 oz/½ cup unrefined golden caster (superfine) sugar, for the caramel

5 organic eggs

175 g/6 oz/¾ cup unrefined golden caster (superfine) sugar or maple sugar

250 g/9 oz/1 cup unsweetened pumpkin purée (page 77), fresh or canned (not to be confused with pumpkin pie filling)

325 ml/11 fl oz/1¼ cups rice milk or almond milk

115 ml/4 fl oz/½ cup coconut milk

1 teaspoon vanilla extract

2½ teaspoons pumpkin spice or allspice

pinch of sea salt (optional)

Preheat the oven to 180°C/350°F/gas mark 4. Put the sugar for the caramel into a saucepan and melt over a medium heat. Let it become golden, then quickly take it off the heat – it will continue to cook from the heat of the pan so you need to work fast. Pour the caramel into a 20 cm/8 inch cake tin or 6 ramekins and tilt the tin to spread the caramel before it hardens. Don't panic if it doesn't coat the entire surface – it will melt in the oven.

Prepare a water bath by taking a deep baking tin larger than the tin used for the caramel, and pouring boiling water into it. Place it in the oven.

In a large mixing bowl, whisk together the eggs and the remaining sugar, then add the pumpkin purée and all the other ingredients and stir until smooth and creamy. Pour the mixture on top of the caramel and place the tin or ramekins in the prepared water bath. The water needs to come three-quarters of the way up the sides of the tin. Bake in the preheated oven for about 25–30 minutes. The flan will be set but not hard – resist cooking it for longer. Remove it from the water bath and let it cool, then put it in the refrigerator for at least 3 hours or overnight.

To unmould, simply run the tip of a small knife along the sides of the tin or ramekins, place your serving dish on top and gently flip over. Gently help it along with the knife and the flan will slip away, golden caramel, spices, creaminess and all!

Ice in Heaven

This is a delicate Persian custard laced with rosewater and sprinkled with pistachios. I love to serve it after something substantial like mutton stew. It is traditionally made with milk, but I've substituted rice milk and you can also use almond milk with good results.

SERVES 6

900 ml/32 fl oz/4 cups rice milk or almond milk

175 g/6 oz/¾ cup golden caster (superfine) sugar

85 g/3 oz/¾ cup rice flour

5 cardamom pods, lightly crushed

2 tablespoons rosewater

2 tablespoons slivered pistachios

rose petals (optional)

Put the rice milk, sugar and flour into a pan. Place over medium low heat until the sugar dissolves and the mixture starts to thicken, about 10 minutes, stirring constantly and making sure your spoon reaches the bottom of the pan so that the mixture doesn't catch. Add the cardamom and rosewater and continue cooking and stirring until the custard is thick and glossy, about another 2 minutes. The custard will resemble a crème patissière. Remove the cardamom pods from the custard, then pour it into ramekins or a heatproof bowl and sprinkle with slivered pistachios and rose petals.

Raw Truffles

These addictive sweets are shaped like truffles but they're actually a mixture of nuts and fruits that can sometimes be better than chocolate! I know, I can't believe I've said that myself, but they have a special taste and texture that you find yourself craving again and again.

MAKES 12–14 LARGE TRUFFLES

150 g/5 oz/1 cup raw almond butter or cashew butter

115 g/4 oz/1 cup raw walnuts or cashews, coarsely chopped

70 g/ 2½ oz/½ cup pitted dried dates, chopped

75 ml/3 fl oz/⅓ cup maple syrup

desiccated coconut/sesame seeds/hulled hemp seeds for rolling

Purée the nut butter, nuts, dates and maple syrup in a food processor until smooth.

Scoop out walnut-sized chunks and roll them between your palms to make round balls. Roll them in either coconut, sesame seeds or hemp seeds. Leave to chill in the refrigerator before serving.

Variations

You can use any nuts you like such as pistachio, hemp, macadamia and adjust the sweetness to your liking by adding or reducing the amount of maple syrup.

Baklava Parcels

Yum! Crispy sticky sweet baklava that's a snip to make and gluten- and dairy-free. Life is good. I was ecstatic when I used rice paper wrappers in the same way as filo pastry and was rewarded with fairly similar results, although the rice paper isn't as crisp. Please make sure you don't use too much oil to brush the parcels, as they have a tendency to become greasy. You can omit the fruits and just use extra nuts, but I love the flavour combination.

MAKES 4

75 ml/2½ fl oz/⅓ cup coconut oil or margarine or ghee

60 g/2 oz/½ cup slivered pistachios

60 g/2 oz/½ cup slivered or sliced almonds

115 g/4 oz/½ cup unrefined golden caster (superfine) sugar, plus extra for sprinkling

⅓ teaspoon ground cardamom (optional)

3–4 saffron threads or pinch saffron powder

1 green apple or 2 red plums, sliced thinly

8 rice paper wrappers

115 ml/4 fl oz/½ cup agave nectar

½ teaspoon orange blossom water

Preheat the oven to 180°C/350°F/gas mark 4. Prepare a baking tray lined with a silicon liner or lightly greased nonstick baking parchment.

Melt the coconut oil or margarine or ghee and let it cool. In a pestle and mortar or a food processor, crush or pulse the pistachios and almonds with the sugar, cardamom (if using) and saffron until you have a crumbly, chunky mixture.

Soak the rice paper wrappers in some water in a shallow dish until soft, about 1 minute. Soften them individually so that they don't end up sticking together. Place them on a plate and layer them with kitchen paper to remove excess water.

Prepare everything so that it's easy to assemble the baklavas. Start by taking 2 wrappers for each baklava. Brush them with a tiny amount of the melted oil, lightly sprinkle them with ½ teaspoon of sugar, and place one on top of the other.

Place 1 tablespoon of the nut mixture in the middle and cover with 3–4 slices of apple or plum. Gather and bunch the wrapper up like a parcel and tie a piece of aluminium foil or thread around it. Place it on the prepared baking tray and move on to the next one. Once done, very lightly brush the tops with some more melted oil and sprinkle the remaining sugar and nut mixture on top. Crinkle them up a bit so that they'll look pretty and even once they are cooked.

Bake in the preheated oven for about 35–45 minutes or until golden. Mix the agave nectar with the orange blossom water. Take the baklavas out of the oven and immediately drizzle them with the agave nectar mixture. (You can also use a 2:1 sugar-to-water Simple Syrup page 158). Try to soak the bottoms more than the tops so that they remain crunchy.

5

ice queen

Cool your senses and enjoy a **creamy** ride with these non-dairy desserts. Now you can indulge yourself with churned vanilla Ice Cream at Last!, Nocciola and Chocolate Ice Cream, and **light** yet filling Konnyaku Noodle Granita. Be creative. Add candy bars and drizzle **variations** of toppings (see Top It Off for some inspiring ideas!) Just remember the following **tips** if you want be an ice queen. Start with the basic ice cream recipe. Once you feel confident, try out the rest. If you have time, allow the mixture to rest in the fridge overnight for the **flavours** to intensify. Leave the ice cream to stand out of the freezer for about 5 minutes to **soften** slightly before serving. Lastly, never take ice cream for granted again!

Cabernet Sauvignon Red Wine Gelato

This is one of the easiest desserts you can make. Once frozen, you can scoop the mixture into silicon moulds in various shapes such as pyramids, hearts or squares, and put it back into the freezer to harden. I like to serve the gelato with warm Molten Chocolate Cake (page 78). Or you can spoon it into small shot glasses and serve them on their own at the end of a dinner, while your guests are still enjoying their drinks.

SERVES 6-8

350 g/12 oz/1½ cups unrefined golden caster (superfine) sugar or 175 ml/6 fl oz/1⅓ cups agave nectar

350 ml/12 fl oz/1½ cups water

350 ml/12 fl oz/1½ cups red wine

225 ml/8 fl oz/1 cup fresh orange juice

350 ml/12 fl oz/1½ cups fresh or frozen raspberry purée

1 tablespoon crème de cassis (optional)

juice of 1 lemon

1 teaspoon vanilla extract

Boil the sugar with the water, stirring until all the sugar has melted. Add the rest of the ingredients and boil for about a minute.

Leave to cool, then put in the refrigerator to infuse overnight, then pour into an ice cream machine and freeze to the manufacturer's instructions. If you don't have an ice cream maker, freeze the mixture for a few hours until hard, then cut it up into chunks and whizz in a food processor until smooth. Then refreeze for another hour.

Once frozen, either place the ice cream in moulds or shot glasses and freeze until hard. You can also place it in a container and let it harden slightly before scooping it out.

Nocciola and Chocolate Ice Cream

Ice cream that is like Nutella but creamier! I used Homemade 'Nutella' (page 157), as it is healthier but just as yummy. Serve this with grilled hazelnuts, Chocolate Sauce (page 144) and a crunchy cookie. It will be your new favourite dessert.

SERVES 4

200 g/7 oz dark (bittersweet) chocolate (minimum 70% cocoa solids) such as Gianduja, finely chopped

70 g/2½ oz/⅓ cup Homemade 'Nutella' (page 157)

tiniest pinch of sea salt (optional)

45 g/1½ oz/¼ cup powdered dairy-free milk such as Vance's, or rice milk powder

800 ml/38 fl oz/3½ cups rice or almond milk

70 g/2½ oz/⅓ cup unrefined golden caster (superfine) sugar

Place the chocolate, 'Nutella', salt (if using) and milk powder in a large bowl and set aside. Bring the rice or almond milk and sugar to the boil in a saucepan. Pour the hot liquid over the chocolate mixture in stages, whisking all the while until all the chocolate has melted.

Leave the mixture in the refrigerator overnight, then pour it into an ice cream machine and follow the manufacturers instructions. If you don't have an ice cream maker, freeze the mixture for a few hours until hard, then cut it up into chunks and whizz in a food processor until smooth. Then refreeze for another hour before serving.

Variations

You can add chopped candied orange peel, nuts or even macerated dried cherries in rum for a whole different take.

Coconut and Lemongrass Sorbet

I picked up this recipe in Thailand on a trip with my husband, Paul. The waiters, wearing great big straw hats, would offer the sorbets to guests who were lounging around by the pool. The refreshing ice-cold sorbets came in straw covered cups hung from bamboo. We were so charmed by these smiling waiters and their lovely sorbets, until we realized that we were being charged £6 a cup for them... small cups at that! After that I made it my mission to get the recipe so that we can all enjoy it at home!

SERVES 4

1 sprig lemongrass

400 ml/14 fl oz/1²⁄₃ cups (1 can) coconut milk

400 ml/14 fl oz/1²⁄₃ cups (1 can) coconut juice

120 g/4 oz/¹⁄₂ cup unrefined golden caster (superfine) sugar

Cut out the tough part of the lemongrass and chop the rest in fine rings. Place the coconut milk, coconut juice, lemongrass and sugar in a pan and bring to the boil. Lower the heat and simmer for about 1 minute, then turn off the heat and allow the milk to cool. You can either put it in the refrigerator overnight for the flavours to intensify before transferring it to your ice cream machine, or use it straight away. It really depends on how quickly you want to eat it. Either way, before pouring it into the machine, strain out the lemongrass. Churn the mixture following the manufacturer's instructions and freeze it for about 1 hour before serving.

If you don't have an ice cream maker, freeze the mixture for a few hours until hard, then cut it up into chunks and whizz in a food processor until smooth. Then refreeze for 2 hours before serving.

Variations

Now, if you like your sorbet to have a macaroon-like texture, add about 85 g/3 oz/1 cup of lightly toasted unsweetened desiccated coconut before heating the mixture. For another flavour you could add 85 g/3 oz/¹⁄₂ cup of chocolate chips to the milk mixture just before pouring it into the ice cream machine.

Wild Orchid Ice Cream

An enterprising young man by the name of Akbar Mashti came up with this ice cream some fifty years ago. It quickly became the most popular ice cream in Iran and it's still going strong, sold in shops and by street vendors everywhere. I think it's because it truly captures the taste of Persia: crunchy pistachios, heady rosewater, fragrant saffron. The texture is different from other dairy-free ice cream, more stretchy, like a gelato. That's because of the salep, the powdered root of a wild orchid ('Orchis mascula'), which is blended into the custard. It's available from Middle Eastern stores. In Iran, this ice cream is served sandwiched between delicate, almost transparent rice wafers. Biting into these cold fragrant discs is one of the best pleasures in the world.

SERVES 4–6

Use the recipe for Ice Cream at Last! on page 129 as your base, and add the following:

a pinch of saffron dissolved in 1 tablespoon of hot water

½ teaspoon rosewater

2 tablespoons slivered pistachios

½ teaspoon salep powder

Tangy Green Apple Sorbet

One of the best sorbets I've ever had was in an ice cream shop called Crispinie in Rome. It was an apple sorbet with the true fresh taste of apples. There were a lot of people waiting their turn, and since I felt a bit rushed I chose a chocolate sorbet as my second scoop along with the apple one. Odd choice, you may say, but the flavours really complemented each other. One fruity and a tad acidic, as green apples should be, the other deep, dark and sweet. Try a little Chocolate Sauce (page 144) with this apple sorbet and see if you like it.

SERVES 4–6

5 medium Granny Smith apples, cored and thinly sliced

juice of 1 lemon

400 ml/14 fl oz/1²⁄₃ cups filtered water

150 g/5 oz/²⁄₃ cups unrefined golden caster (superfine) sugar

60 ml/2 fl oz/¹⁄₄ cup agave nectar

dash of Calvados, optional

(Note: You can replace the sugar, water and agave nectar with about 525–550 ml/18–19 fl oz/ 1¹⁄₄–1¹⁄₂ cups of Simple Syrup page 158)

Put the apples into a bowl and toss them with the lemon juice. Transfer them to a ziplock bag, or wrap the bowl tightly with clingfilm, and put in the freezer overnight or until the apples are frozen solid. This step ensures that the apples, once puréed, will retain their colour.

In a saucepan over medium heat, boil the water and sugar together for 3–4 minutes. Take off the heat and allow the syrup to cool before adding the agave nectar. If using pre-made simple syrup, omit this step and just mix the agave nectar straight in.

Blend the frozen apples in a food processor with 20 ml/6 fl oz/½ cup of the simple syrup until you get a very fine and smooth purée. If the purée has large specks of skin in it, blend for a bit longer, otherwise once frozen the skins will be too tough. Add the rest of the syrup and the Calvados – about 2 teaspoons or more depending on your taste – and blend for a few more seconds. Pour the mixture into your ice cream machine, and freeze according to the manufacturer's instructions. If you don't have an ice cream maker, freeze the mixture for a few hours until hard, then cut it up into chunks and whizz in a food processor until smooth. Then refreeze for another hour before serving.

'Like Water for Chocolate' Sorbet

This recipe will satisfy all your chocolate cravings in one go! I use Caraïbe 66% cocoa solids chocolate from Valrhona, as it has hints of dried fruits and grilled almonds. For a bolder taste, go for a 70% cocoa solids chocolate instead. If you can't get Valrhona, try Green and Black's organic chocolate. Serve the sorbet with a coulis of passion fruit, mango or raspberries. You can also spoon the prepared sorbet in its soft stage into silicon moulds and let them harden. For a sophisticated smooth finish, pour some Chocolate Sauce (page 144) on top after you remove it from the freezer.

SERVES 4

450 ml/18 fl oz/2 cups filtered or mineral water

225 g/½ lb Caraïbe chocolate, chopped

175 g/6 oz/¾ cup unrefined golden caster (superfine) sugar

Heat the water with the chocolate and sugar until boiling. Take off the heat and let it cool completely before pouring it into the ice cream machine. If you don't have an ice cream maker, freeze the mixture for a few hours until hard, then cut it up into chunks and whizz in a food processor until smooth. Then refreeze for another hour.

If you'd like to cover the sorbet with a layer of Chocolate Ganache (page 144), take it out of its mould when it's frozen and place it on a wire rack, with a plate underneath to catch the excess glaze. Make sure the sorbet is rock hard before you start, so that it doesn't melt while you are working with it. Take a small ladle and fill it up with the sauce. Starting from the top of the ice cream, pour over the chocolate sauce quickly and in one big swoop, allowing it to fall generously so that it covers the edges. Immediately tap the wire rack several times to burst any trapped air bubbles, so that you're left with a silky smooth finish.

Decorate the top with a gold or silver leaf and serve immediately. Otherwise, you can put the glazed ice cream back in the freezer and serve at a later time.

Bright Mango Sorbet

This sorbet is a simple combination of fresh mangoes and sugar, with a little lime juice to balance the sweetness. Fix the sugar according to your own taste, but remember that everything will taste sweeter before it's put into the freezer – the taste of all things frozen is always more subdued. Serve it with a scoop of Coconut and Lemongrass Sorbet (page 118) for a tropical treat.

SERVES 4

225 ml/9 fl oz/1 cup Simple Syrup (page 158)

2 tablespoons agave nectar

1 kg/2¼ lbs fresh mangoes, peeled
and chopped

115 ml/4 fl oz/½ cup fresh lime juice

Boil the syrup and agave nectar for about 5 minutes. Allow it to cool. Meanwhile, purée the mangoes and lime juice in a blender or food processor until smooth. Mix the syrup and the purée together, then immediately pour into an ice cream machine and churn. If you don't have an ice cream maker, freeze the mixture for a few hours until hard, then cut it up into chunks and whizz in a food processor until smooth.

Put into a container, cover with clingfilm and leave in the freezer for at least 4 hours before serving.

Vegan Vanilla Ice Cream

No eggs, cream or milk. What's left, you might ask! This ice cream is a concoction of almond or rice milk, powdered milk alternative, gelatine or agar agar and a few other simple ingredients.

You can use this as a base for other flavours: see Ice Cream Variations, page 130. Clean and smooth, it's light, refreshing and creamy even though it's extremely low in fat.

SERVES 4–6

1 vanilla pod
675 ml/24 fl oz/3 cups rice milk or almond milk
115 g/4 oz/½ cup unrefined golden caster (superfine) sugar
2 tablespoons grapeseed oil or ghee

45 g/1½ oz/¼ cup Vance's DariFree milk powder + 60 ml/2 fl oz/½ cup filtered water (you can substitute these for 225 ml/8 fl oz/ 1 cup coconut cream instead)
½ tablespoon agar agar flakes, or 4 gelatine leaves (soaked in water until soft, then the excess water squeezed out)

Split the vanilla pod in half and place in a pan with the milk, sugar, oil and water. Bring to the boil. Lower the heat, add the agar agar flakes and cook for about 2 minutes, stirring constantly with a whisk. If using gelatine leaves, boil the liquid for 2 minutes, remove from the heat and then add the gelatine leaves.

Remove from the heat, add the DariFree milk powder and whisk again, making sure there are no lumps. If there are, simply pour the mixture into a blender or food processor and whizz for a few seconds.

Let the mixture cool to room temperature, then remove the vanilla pod, scrape out the seeds and add them to the mixture. Pour into an ice cream machine and freeze according to the manufacturer's instructions.If you don't have an ice cream maker, freeze the mixture for a few hours until hard, then cut it up into chunks and whizz in a food processor until smooth. Then refreeze for another hour before serving.

Pink Champagne Granita

We all know that Champagne is the wine of celebration. It has toasted special occasions from the launching of ships to grand prix, weddings and endless parties. There are many very good sparkling wines, but only a few are allowed to be called Champagne and they are the ones grown specifically in the region of Champagne in France. In 1688, Don Perignon, a monk in charge of the monastery cellars there, was responsible for laying the foundation for Champagne when a mistake in the fermentation process led to bubbles. The house of Möet, founded in 1743, and subsequently Cliquot, improved the Champagne, the size of its bubbles, the bottles and the corks, to what we have today.

This granita can be served as a palate cleanser between meals, or as a dessert. It is quite strong – a serving is equivalent to a glass of Champagne. You don't need to use a Crystal or even a Dom for this recipe. Choose a Veuve Cliquot, Taittinger or Moët. In fact, you don't have to use Champagne at all – if you prefer, you can use your favourite sparkling wine instead. This recipe is perfect for that bottle of Champagne opened the day before that's gone slightly flat and you're not sure what to do with it.

SERVES 4–6

> 900 ml/32 fl oz/4 cups rosé champagne
>
> 5–6 tablespoons icing sugar
>
> 1 tablespoon fresh lemon juice

Stir the Champagne, icing sugar and lemon juice together in a bowl. Place in the freezer and stir with a fork every 20 minutes until it's frozen. Don't worry if it's rock hard when you take it out – by the time you serve it at the table it will have reached the perfect consistency.

If you like you can garnish it with a few berries, sprigs of mint or even rose petals.

Ice Cream at Last!

Ice cream is one of my favourite desserts. When my family and I lived in New York back in the early '80s, Häagen-Dazs, before it became a super-brand, was our local ice cream store! As a kid I would dream of owning a giant ice cream factory and later, as a pastry chef, I came up with designer signature sundaes with an array of flavours, textures and toppings. Needless to say, I was shattered to learn that my stomach could no longer accept the daily dairy intake. Since I'm severely allergic to soya, I couldn't even eat the usual dairy-free ice cream, and I was pretty sceptical about using watery rice milk when coming up with this recipe. It took me days, plus many cartons of eggs and packets of sugar, but it was all worth it. This is ice cream that'll blow you away! It's also a perfect base for other flavours.

SERVES 4–6

1 x recipe Crème Anglaise (page 147)

40 g/1½ oz unrefined golden caster (superfine) sugar

2 gelatine leaves

Follow the method for making crème anglaise on page 147 and add the extra sugar.

While the crème anglaise is cooking, place the sheets of gelatine in some iced water, enough to cover them. Let them 'bloom' or soften completely, about 5 minutes. Pick them up with your fingers and gently squeeze the excess water out of them. Then prepare a bain-marie by setting a small bowl inside a larger bowl filled with ice.

As soon as you remove the crème anglaise from the heat, add the gelatine, whisk again and place in the bain-marie. Set aside and leave the mixture to cool until it reaches room temperature.

If you'd like the ice cream to gather more flavour, let it rest in the refrigerator overnight. Pour the crème anglaise into the ice cream machine and freeze according to the manufacturers instructions. If you don't have an ice cream maker, freeze the mixture for a few hours until hard, then cut it up into chunks and whizz in a food processor until smooth and refreeze.

Once frozen, store in the freezer for a couple of hours before devouring. Just make sure to take it out of the freezer a few minutes before serving as the ice cream can get a little hard due to the its relatively low fat content.

Remember, this can also be used just like a crème anglaise which has less sugar, served over hot apple pie, puddings and fruit tarts.

Ice Cream Variations

There are endless variations on Ice Cream At Last! Some ingredients need to be blended or whisked into the warm custard, while others can be folded in right before churning or immediately afterwards.

STRAWBERRY DREAM

Clean 250 g/9 oz of fresh strawberries and purée them in a blender or food processor until smooth. Place the purée in a pan and cook over medium heat for about 10 minutes. Let it cool, then whisk into the prepared custard and churn in your machine.

VANILLA FUDGE BROWNIE

Take about 2 x 7 cm/3 inch brownie squares (page 74) and crumble them up with your fingers. Mix into your prepared ice cream. Freeze the ice cream again before serving.

DULCE DE LECHE

Follow the recipe for Ice Cream At Last!, omitting 40 g/1½ oz of the sugar. Add 120 g/4 oz of Dulce de Leche (page 142) at room temperature, to the churned ice cream. Fold in gently so you can see the swirls and refreeze.

ROCKY ROAD

Chop 60 g/2 oz chocolate and 5–6 marshmallows into 1 cm/½ inch squares. Roughly chop about 60 g/2 oz almonds and mix everything together. Once the ice cream has come out of the machine, fold in the chopped ingredients and allow the ice cream to harden in the freezer for a couple of hours.

CHESTNUT

Omit 60 g/2 oz/¼ cup of sugar from the custard base, and whisk in 75 g/2½ oz/⅓ cup of sweetened chestnut purée to the warm custard. Cool, then add 4–5 chopped candied chestnuts and churn in the ice cream machine.

MACHA

As in the recipe for Créme Anglaise (page 147), simply add 2 teaspoons of powdered green tea or a few green tea leaves to the boiling milk (see Ice Cream At Last!), omitting the vanilla pod. Follow the rest of the recipe but remember to strain the custard before pouring it into the machine.

ROASTED ALMOND

Roast 60 g/2 oz/½ cup of almond nibs in a dry pan or in the oven until lightly brown. Let them cool to room temperature. Meanwhile, mix 1½ teaspoons of salep powder with about 4–5 tablespoons of the cold custard. Whisk vigorously into the rest of the custard, add the almonds and pour into the ice cream machine.

Blue Agave Tequila Sorbet

A cool sorbet with the warming taste of tequila and lime juice, sweetened with its own nectar, the agave syrup. Nothing will get in the way of you and this incredible taste. The Aztecs were making a sacred alcoholic beverage from the blue agave plant long before the Spanish came and refined it into the tequila we know today. The agave plant is spiked with swordlike leaves with a core shaped like a pineapple, which is distilled to make 'aguamiel' (honey water) and then turned into tequila. Although it may look like a big beautiful blue cactus or aloe plant, the agave in fact belongs to the lily family.

The key to good tequila lies in the agave's harvesting. The plant needs to be harvested by hand when it is perfectly ripe, anywhere from eight to twelve years old. The name of the plant comes from the Greek word for 'noble' or 'admirable', although we all know how unlike that we can be after one too many tequila shots! OK, here's how to enjoy your shots a different way. Start with the best tequila you can get your hands on, one labelled 100% blue agave, such as a Reposado (rested in oak barrels for at least two months and up to a year), or a fresh-tasting Blanco (white or silver), which has a clean fresh taste straight from the still. However, if you can't get one of these, just use your favourite tequila.

SERVES 2–4

450 ml/16 fl oz/2 cups filtered water

115 ml/4 fl oz/½ cup agave nectar

2 gelatine leaves, softened in water

150 ml/5 fl oz/⅔ cup lime juice

75 ml/2½ fl oz/⅓ cup tequila

tiniest pinch of sea salt

Make a syrup with the water and agave nectar by simply letting the mixture come to the boil and then turning off the heat. Squeeze the water out of the gelatine leaves and place them in the hot syrup. They will dissolve with the residual heat. Pour in the lime juice, then the tequila and salt, and allow the mixture to cool completely. Pour into an ice cream machine and churn. Place the sorbet in the freezer and let it harden slightly before serving. If you don't have an ice cream machine, pour the liquid mixture into a container and freeze. Break into chunks and pulse in a food processor or blender until you get a smooth slush-like mixture. Freeze again for a good hour or more before serving.

Serve the sorbet as you would margaritas, in a glass with a sliver of lime for decoration, or in large shot glasses rimmed with sugar.

Konnyaku and Lime Noodle Granita

Also known as Faloudeh, this seems to be one of the very first iced desserts known to man. In 400BC, Persian engineers had created the way to store ice in the middle of the summer, in the desert heat. Giant chunks of ice were carried from nearby mountains and stored in enormous underground rooms by the name of yakh-chals (ice storage). These rooms were then connected to a series of wind-catchers, which kept them at icy levels. The ice created in these spaces was then used by palace cooks to create desserts such as this one, the Faloudeh, an icy concoction of crunchy noodles, saffron, fruits and other flavours, only served to royalties. It is still eaten today, sometimes drizzled with sour cherry syrup or a squeeze of lime juice. A truly refreshing and unusual dessert.

SERVES 4–6

500 g/16 oz konnyaku noodles, chopped up, or very thin rice noodles, broken into small 3 cm/1¼ inch pieces

430 g/1 lb/2 cups unrefined golden caster (superfine) sugar

160 ml/6 fl oz/⅔ cup filtered water

80 ml/3 fl oz/⅓ cup lime juice

1 tablespoon rosewater

If using konnyaku noodles, blanch them quickly in boiling water, then run them under ice-cold water and strain out the excess. If using rice noodles, boil them in water for 1 minute, then strain and run ice-cold water over them.

Boil the sugar, water and lime juice until the sugar dissolves. Let the liquid cool. Add the noodles and the rosewater to the cooled sugar and water mixture, and churn in the ice cream machine. You can also pour the mixture into a tray, freeze for 30 minutes, and fluff the ice with a fork. Repeat twice more, then let the mixture freeze for a few hours or overnight.

Serve with a drizzle of sour cherry syrup or extra lime wedges.

Creamy Cashew Nut Ice Cream

You'll need pure, raw, unroasted, unsalted cashew nuts as the base for this delicious ice cream. The first time I had something similar was at the Natural Food Expo in California – I polished off all the samples at one company's stand and kept shaking my head, asking, 'Are you sure there's no dairy in this?' In fact they were so conscious of not using dairy in their foods that they didn't allow anything non-vegan to come within a few metres of their stand. Lovely creamy cashew nut soft-serve ice cream!

SERVES 2–4

1 vanilla pod

450 ml/16 fl oz/2 cups coconut juice or rice milk or almond milk

175 ml/6 fl oz/¾ cup agave nectar

or 225 ml/8 fl oz/1 cup maple syrup

225 g/8 oz/2 cups raw cashew nuts or 250 g/8 oz/1 cup Cashew Nut 'Butter' (page 150)

Cut the vanilla pod in half and scrape out the seeds. Add the seeds to the coconut juice, rice milk or almond milk. Pour into a blender or food processor, add the agave nectar or maple syrup and the cashew nuts, and blend until smooth. If using cashew nut butter, simply mix the ingredients together with a whisk or spoon. Place in an ice cream machine and churn, or transfer to a container, freeze, then break into chunks and blend in a food processor. You may need to freeze the mixture for about an hour before serving.

Variations

You can replace the liquid part of the recipe by fruit juices such as peach, apple, strawberry, mango, even coconut milk for extra creaminess. Reduce the sugar by as much as half and follow the method above.

Iced Entremets (Ice Cream Cakes)

Who says the only way to serve ice creams and sorbets is to scoop them into serving dishes? How about serving them as a cake? Even better, as a layered cake with different textures and colours? This is by far one of the easiest desserts and yields the prettiest presentation.

You need a flan ring or a silicon mould, and you can make one large ice cake or several individual ones. The principle is basically the same as Tropical Fruit Mousse (page 94), but using ice cream instead of mousse. To give you a better idea of the general principle: line a flan ring or mould with thinly cut cake, soak the cake with some syrup, add a layer of ice cream, then a layer of fruit purée or crushed nuts or both, and cover again with some ice cream. Unmould and flip on to a serving plate or dish, and decorate the top. You can use different-flavoured ice creams or sorbets in the same cake if you like.

This dessert is super easy but does need to be planned ahead. The ice cream base needs to be made and churned and the rest is all about assembling. When the cake is made it needs to be stored in the freezer, but it can be taken out to be the perfect party dessert at a moment's notice.

SERVES 6–8

Joconde

150 g/5 oz/1¼ cups ground almonds

45 g/1½ oz/⅓ cup gluten-free flour

115 g/4 oz/1 cup icing (confectioners') sugar

4 organic eggs + 4 egg whites

60 g/2 oz/¼ cup unrefined golden granulated sugar

30 g/1 oz margarine or ghee or coconut butter, melted and cooled

1 x recipe Simple Syrup (page 158)

115 g/4 oz/1 cup chopped fruits or nuts

Dr Oetker's glaze or 1 x recipe Dark Chocolate Ganache (page 144)

Preheat the oven to 220°C/425°F/gas mark 7. Line two 30 x 20 cm/12 x 8 inch swiss roll trays with baking parchment, lightly brushed with melted coconut butter or ghee.

Sift the ground almonds, flour and icing sugar into a bowl and set aside. In a KitchenAid fitted with a whisk attachment, whisk all the egg whites until foamy, then add the granulated sugar in stages until you get stiff peaks. Set aside and whisk the egg yolks until pale and creamy, about 3 minutes. Fold in the flour mixture until just incorporated, then mix in the melted margarine, ghee or coconut butter. Fold in the meringue, making sure not to over-blend. Spread on to the prepared trays using a spatula. The best way to do this is to pour the whole lot on to the middle of the tray, spread it in an X to the four corners of the tray, then fill in the gaps. Bake in the preheated oven for about 5–7 minutes or until golden. Turn the trays over on to a clean piece of baking parchment and remove the paper from the cakes.

Using a 20 cm/8 inch flan or cake ring, cut out two circles, then two strips along the length of the cakes about the same width as the sides of the flan ring, so that when joined they will go round the inside of the flan ring. Place the flan ring on a tray lined with baking parchment. Put one cake layer inside the ring and brush with syrup. Place the strips on the inside of the ring, brush with syrup, then add some ice cream and top with another layer of cake. Soak in more syrup. Add your chopped fruits or nuts. Top with ice cream and smooth with a spatula. Place the cake in the freezer. Meanwhile, prepare the glaze according to the instructions, or make some ganache. Decorate the set ice cream and serve.

Sundaes

The sundae dates as far back as 1892, and there are many claims as to who came up with it first. Although it's not rocket science, it does get people very excited, even astronauts.

"I'm still saving a hot fudge sundae for you." **NASA administrator Goldin to US astronaut Norm Thagard, upon his return from a three-and-a-half-month stint aboard Space Station Mir.**

Don't wait too long before you have a sundae. Have fun with it. Use left-over cakes, sauces, brittles, chopped-up candy bars, jelly, fresh fruits and come up with your own signature dessert. Decorate with sugar crystals, Mock Whipped Cream (page148), or sliced fruits.

Here are some of my favourite combinations; feel free to add as much or as little topping as you like. There are no rules when it comes to something as delicious as this. All these sundaes are made with 2 scoops of ice cream and layered with different ingredients. Start by adding a spoonful of sauce or coulis to the bottom of the serving dish to create a yummy pool, then alternate with the rest of the ingredients. Try to finish the sundae with a little of each ingredient as decoration. It will make them look appetizing as well as giving your guests a little hint to what's in them.

MONT BLANC

A winning combination. Layer 2 scoops of vanilla ice cream with 2 tablespoons of chestnut purée, 2 rounded tablespoons of lightly crushed meringue and 4 rounded tablespoons of Mock Whipped Cream (page 148) folded with 3 tablespoons Crème Patissèrie (page 146).

MANGO MADNESS

Layer 2 scoops of Bright Mango Sorbet (page 124) with 3 tablespoons of chopped sun-dried mangoes, some raspberry coulis and 2 tablespoons of crushed macadamia nuts.

LEMONCELLO

Lemon explosion. Layer 2 scoops of vanilla ice cream with 3 tablespoons of Luscious Lemon Cream (page 152) mixed with layers of 1 tablespoon of Limoncello liqueur, 1½ tablespoon of lightly roasted slivered almonds, 4 tablespoons of fresh lemon jelly, roughly chopped up.

PURE MILK

No one will ever guess that there is no dairy in this sundae. Layer 2 scoops vanilla ice cream, 3 tablespoons of Dulce de Leche (see page 142) and 2 tablespoons of Crème Patissèrie (page 146) whisked with 3 tablespoons Mock Whipped Cream (page 148).

CHOCOCONUT

Like a yummy Bounty bar. Layer 2 scoops of chocolate sorbet with 2 crushed-up Coconut Rochers (page 24), 3 tablespoons of Chocolate Sauce and 2 tablespoons of Dark Chocolate Ganache (page 145) at room temperature. Top with chocolate shavings and lightly roasted coconut slivers.

6

top it off

dulce de leche

Who says you have to use dairy or soya to make your **favourite toppings**, like fluffy Mock Whipped Cream, vanilla-flecked Crème Patissière and Dark Chocolate Ganache? No more longing for Dulce de Leche! These beauties can top your desserts as decorations; they can be **crumbled** into cake mixtures, **folded** into mousses, **spread** and piped on cakes and **drizzled** on sundaes. They can be the foundation for yummy desserts such as ice creams and tarts. They keep desserts together with their fluffiness, sweetness and crunch. They add **zing**, colour, depth and **flavour** wherever you need it. These toppings deliver that **extra something** you thought you could only get through conventional ingredients such as butter, cream and soya milk or tofu. You'll see that coconut cream, nut and rice milks, agave nectar and nut butters make **perfect** substitutes. Who would have thought that a **dollop** of heavenly sweetness here and a **sprinkle** of crunch there was all you needed to top off the **perfect** alternative dessert?

Dulce de Leche

If you've ever tasted this South American caramel then you know just how amazingly addictive it is. You also know that you can't eat it if you're dairy intolerant as it is made with cow or goat's milk that has been stirred over a low heat for hours and hours until caramelized.

The one I made here is incredibly similar and takes less than a few minutes to make. Light, almost whipped milky caramel with a delicate stretch. I top ice creams with it, whisk into my butter creams and sometimes, I just simply eat it straight up with a spoon.

MAKES APPROX 250 G/8 OZ/2 CUPS

250 g/9 oz/1½ cups unrefined light brown sugar

325 ml/11 fl oz/1⅓ cups coconut milk

115 g/4 oz/½ cup margarine or ghee at room temperature

Place the sugar in a heavy saucepan with 3 tablespoons water and cook over a medium high heat until it starts to melt around the sides. Occasionally stir the sugar with a wooden spoon for about 5–7 minutes until most of the sugar dissolves and you see only a few small lumps. The caramel will be a little darker than when you first melted it. Remove the pan from the heat and pour in the coconut milk, but be careful as it may splash a bit. Put the pan back on the stove and lower the heat slightly. Stir out any remaining lumps then turn off the heat once you get a smooth caramel. It should have taken on a lovely dark amber colour. Set it aside and leave to cool a bit. After several minutes, check its temperature and if it is warm to the touch, add the soft ghee or margarine in stages and stir with a fork or small whisk until it disappears into the caramel.

Place in the refrigerator. Once the dulce de leche is cold, take a fork or mini whisk and vigorously whisk the caramel for about 1–2 minutes. You can also use a hand-held electric whisk. The caramel will lighten considerably in colour and become creamier and slightly fluffier in texture, like a real dulce de leche! Store in an airtight container in the refrigerator.

Note: your cooled caramel must have a slight stretch to it, not be dry in texture like fudge. If it has 'seized', then simply add about 2 tablespoons coconut milk to the caramel and heat briefly in the microwave or on the stove until hot and bubbly. Pour back into a bowl and cool in the refrigerator before whisking.

Fruit Coulis

Ever wondered how to give your desserts that restaurant finish? Well, here's one of the tricks of the trade. These fruit sauces are light and colourful. They add flavour and sparkle to any dessert and are a quick way of turning an ordinary dish into one that looks as if it's been plated in a top class eaterie.. Almost any juicy fruit can be puréed into a coulis. Choose fruits that are just ripe but not overly soft. The amount of sugar you add really depends on how sweet the fruit is in the first place, and also on your tastebuds. The measurements below are just a guideline, so experiment to see how much sugar you like. These recipes are made with Simple Syrup (page 158). If you don't have any in stock, simply use equal amounts of icing (confectioners') sugar blended with hot water. For a low-carb and low-glycaemic version I like to use light agave nectar instead of sugar, which also has no aftertaste.

MAKES APPROX 375 G/12 OZ/1 CUP

STRAWBERRY

Take 300 g/10 oz cut strawberries and purée with 5 tablespoons of Simple Syrup (page 158) or 2 tablespoons of agave nectar mixed with 1 tablespoon of water. Pass through a fine-meshed sieve and serve.

RASPBERRY

Take 300 g/10 oz of fresh raspberries, purée with 5 tablespoons of Simple Syrup or 2 tablespoons of agave nectar mixed with 1 tablespoon of water. Pass through a fine-meshed sieve and serve.

MANGO

Take 2 mangoes, purée with 4 tablespoons of Lemongrass Syrup (page 158) or 1½ tablespoons of agave nectar and ½ tablespoon of water, and 1½ tablespoons of lime or lemon juice. Serve immediately.

PLUM AND SAKE

Take 4–5 large red plums, pitted and cut in half, and purée with 50 ml/2 fl oz/½ cup of Simple Syrup. Pass through a fine-meshed sieve, and add 2 tablespoons of saké (or to taste).

Dark Chocolate Ganache

Ganache is a French term referring to a velvety smooth mixture of chocolate and heavy cream that has been around since the 1850s. It has multi-functional properties: it can be chilled, scooped and rolled for truffles, thinned out for glazes, warmed up and used as a thick hot fudge sauce over ice cream, spread between fluffy cakes or piped on top of them as decoration. The ganache can also fill a pastry case for a dense chocolate tart.

MAKES APPROX 275 G/9 OZ/1 CUP

115 ml/4 fl oz/½ cup full-fat coconut milk, or rice milk with 1½ tablespoons margarine or ghee or coconut butter added

115 g/4 oz dark (bittersweet) chocolate with a minimum of 60% cocoa solids, e.g.Valrhona's Guanaja or Caraïbe

3 tablespoons margarine or ghee or coconut butter, at room temperature

Heat the coconut milk to almost boiling and pour over the chopped chocolate. Gently stir with a rubber spatula or wooden spoon without creating any air bubbles. Set aside for about 3–5 minutes, then stir in the margarine or ghee. Cover and refrigerate for at least 2 hours before rolling into balls (see Raw Truffles, page 110).

Chocolate Sauce

This silky smooth sauce is the perfect accompaniment to sundaes, tarts or anything that calls for chocolate sauce.

MAKES APPROX 500 ML/17 FL OZ/ 1 CUP

115 g/4 oz any excellent quality dark (bittersweet) chocolate

175 ml/6 fl oz/¾ cup coconut milk or rice milk with 1½ tablespoons ghee or coconut butter or margarine added

40 g/1½ oz unrefined golden caster (superfine) sugar

Place all the ingredients in a heavy saucepan and bring to the boil. Boil for about 1 minute, then remove from the heat and serve.

Crème Patissière

Luscious, creamy, and just like the real thing. This was one of the desserts I missed most when I found out I was dairy-intolerant. This version is also low in fat, as it uses virtually fat-free rice milk. It's amazingly versatile – you can whisk in softened margarine or ghee or coconut butter to add more depth, fold in a little Mock Whipped Cream (page 148) to lighten it up, or add liqueurs, melted chocolate, fruit purées, pastes and extracts to alter it completely. Whatever you add to this custard, it will still be creamy and sumptuous!

MAKES APPROX 750 G/1½ LB/2 CUPS

450 ml/6 fl oz/2 cups rice milk

1 small vanilla pod, split lengthwise

5 organic egg yolks

85 g/3 oz/⅓ cup unrefined golden caster (superfine) sugar

40 g/1¼ oz/¼ cup cornflour (corn starch)

1 teaspoon Cointreau or kirsch (optional)

Heat the milk with the vanilla pod in a heavy-based saucepan until very hot. Turn off the heat and leave to infuse for about 15 minutes – this way you get the maximum flavour out of the vanilla.

Meanwhile, whisk the egg yolks and sugar until smooth. Add the cornflour and whisk until very pale, about 1 minute or so. Reheat the milk and vanilla and pour over the yolks in three stages, whisking between each addition. Pour the mixture back into the pan and put back on a medium-low heat. Now start whisking gently, all the time watching the liquid get thicker. This can happen very quickly, so don't go anywhere! Keep whisking until the liquid starts to evaporate and it becomes custard-like, making sure your whisk reaches the bottom and sides of the pan. As soon as you see a bubble or two in the middle of the custard, take it off the heat and pour it into a clean bowl. If the custard curdles, which it really won't if you follow this method, don't panic – there's a remedy to hand. Either take the custard off the heat and whisk it as hard as you possibly can, or whizz it (after removing the vanilla) in a food processor. Another method is to strain it.

Take out the vanilla pod, whisk in the Cointreau or kirsch (if using), and cover with clingfilm, making sure that it touches the top of the custard so that no skin forms as it cools. Leave to cool, then chill in the refrigerator for a few hours before using.

Variations

Chocolate Crème Patissière: once the crème is done, remove the pan from the heat and stir in 175 g/6 oz finely chopped dark chocolate. Place in a bowl, cover in clingfilm and refrigerate.

Crème Mousseline: this is creamier version of the crème patissèrie but somehow lighter hence the addition of margarine or ghee. Once the crème patissèrie has cooled to room temperature, place it in a KitchenAid (or other food mixer) fitted with a whisk and start the machine on medium-low. Place 150 g/5 oz softened margarine or ghee into the cream in 3 or 4 additions making sure it is well whipped each time.

Créme Anglaise

A British sauce despite its name and avidly used by French chefs. This recipe uses almost fat-free almond or rice milk as opposed to a classic combination of milk and double (heavy) cream. To add a bit of depth, I've added some ghee or grapeseed oil and a little DariFree milk powder to thicken it up. Dotted with vanilla, this Créme Anglaise is perfect to top tarts, cakes, puddings, fresh fruits and warm pies. It is also the foundation for many ice creams.

MAKES APPROX 250 G/8 OZ/2 CUPS

1 large vanilla pod

500 ml/18 fl oz/ 2 cups rice milk or almond milk (if not using DariFree milk powder, use coconut milk here)

85 g/3 oz/⅓ cup unrefined golden caster (superfine) sugar

pinch of sea salt (optional)

5 organic egg yolks, lightly whisked

45 g/1½ oz/¼ cup Vance's DariFree milk powder

2 tablespoons grapeseed oil or ghee

Slit the vanilla pod along its length and remove the seeds with the back of a knife. Put the seeds, pod, rice milk (or coconut milk) 1 teaspoon of the sugar and salt (if using) in a saucepan and place over a low to medium heat. Try not to let it come to the boil – the sugar will stop the milk spilling over. Remove from the heat, cover the pan and allow to infuse for around 15 minutes. This gets the maximum flavour out of the vanilla pod.

Meanwhile, set aside a medium bowl with a fine-meshed sieve over it, and fill a large bowl with ice.

Remove the vanilla pod, wash it and leave it to dry. (You can either put it in your sugar jar to make vanilla sugar, or grind it to produce heady vanilla powder.)

Whisk the yolks with the rest of the sugar and the DariFree milk powder in a large bowl, then pour in the hot milk, a third at a time – if you add it all at once the eggs will curdle. Whisk continuously and add the grapeseed oil or ghee.

Then return the mixture to the pan, place over a medium-low heat and stir continuously with a wooden spoon until pale and creamy, about 4–5 minutes. This part is crucial. Whatever you do, don't allow it to come to the boil or the mixture will curdle. Be very attentive and watch over it. (If the mixture does curdle, an excellent trick that works with any créme anglaise, dairy-free or otherwise, is to whizz the curdled mixture in a blender or food processor and then strain through a sieve. The créme anglaise will be creamy smooth once again.)

Once you see a lot of steam rising, carefully put your finger in it and if it's too hot to the touch (around 80°C/180°F to be more precise), take it off the heat. Another way to tell if it's ready is to draw your finger over the back of the spoon – it should leave an impression that does not run. (At this point you could turn the mixture into other recipes such as ice cream – see page 129–130.)

Remove the pan from the heat and strain the mixture through the sieve into the medium bowl. You can add a little water to the ice-filled bowl to create an ice-bath. Stand the bowl of crème anglaise over the ice, and stir occasionally until it has cooled completely.

Mock Whipped Cream

So many of my old French recipes rely on whipped cream that when I became dairy-intolerant I was in a dilemma, but one day I tried whisking cold coconut cream and it came up into stiff fluffy peaks – I was on cloud nine! This whipped cream can be folded into Crème Patissèrie (page 146), into mousses of all kinds, used as a topping for ice cream sundaes, pies and fruits. In fact, it can be used with almost anything that calls for whipped cream!

WHIPPED CREAM

Pour a carton of liquid coconut cream (not the solid squares of hard cream) into a bowl and place in the refrigerator until cool – about 1 hour. Whisk until peaks form. (If you have trouble finding coconut cream, place a 400 ml/14 fl oz can of coconut milk in the refrigerator for about 1 hour. Remove it, and without shaking or tilting the can, open it slowly. With a spoon, take out the top layer of the milk, which will be the cream, making sure you leave behind the almost clear liquid underneath.)

Pour the cream into a bowl and whisk until fluffy. Try not to over-whip it, or it will take on a dryish texture. You can add icing (confectioners') sugar and vanilla extract before you whip it, or keep it simple if it is going to be folded into other mixtures.

FLUFFY CREAM USING A PROFI-WHIP MACHINE

Fluffy cream which can be used anywhere whipped cream is called for. Just like the canned dairy whipped cream! Perfect as a topping to your Chocolat Chaud (page 178), Sundaes (page 136), Chocolate Pot au Crème (page 99) or even a simple bowl of strawberries. You can also use it just like the recipe above, on its own, to fold into Tropical Fruit Mousse (page 94) or with Silky Smooth Pumpkin Pie (page 77). I love piping it into layered trifles set in simple individual glasses. Add a few drops of natural food colouring for a funky hue.

CREME CHANTILLY

You will need a Profi Whip whipped cream dispenser for this recipe. Open a 400 ml/14 fl oz can of coconut cream or milk. The latter will give you a lighter cream. Take 100 ml/3½ fl oz/⅓ cup of the milk and ½ teaspoon agar agar, put them in a pan, and stir them together over a low heat for 2–3 minutes. Mix this liquid with the rest of the coconut milk from the can and pour into your Profi Whip dispenser. Place in the refrigerator for about 1 hour before using.

CHOCOLATE MOUSSE

You can enjoy the lightest and loveliest chocolate mousse without the dairy. This recipe brought tears of joy to my eyes! Simply open a 14 oz/400 ml can of full-fat coconut milk or cream. Whisk 3 tablespoons cocoa or carob powder with 4 tablespoons unrefined golden caster sugar and add it to the milk. Whisk until very smooth and chocolatey brown all over. Place into your Profi Whip machine and follow the instructions. Whip into a glass filled with macerated raspberries as chocolate mousses, or use as crème chantilly to top ice cream sundaes or anything else that calls for whipped cream.

Raw Cashew Nut 'Butter'

The raw food movement is taking California by storm and it's heading for our shores! Many of the foods we consider fun foods have, in fact, come from the West Coast – with its abundance of fruits and vegetables and mixture of world cultures, plus its laid-back attitude, California is a perfect breeding-ground for new ideas.

Raw food isn't new at all. It started in the '70s, but has now become the hot new diet. Unlike diet fads, though, it is a way of life tied into an uncomplicated philosophy. Raw or live food is organic food that hasn't been heated above 46°C/115°F. To give you an idea, you can actually touch it with your fingers at that temperature. The diet consists of fruits and vegetables, their juices, nuts and seeds as well as their sprouted form. Fruits and vegetables dehydrated either in the oven or by the sun are OK. Tofu is not, as it has been treated, and neither are roasted nut butters. Sushi isn't on the menu either, as it isn't alive. Raw food eaters can have wine, as it has been cold treated, but no other alcohol. Certain sugars are good, such as maple syrup, untreated honey, raw agave nectar and mashed dates. As you can imagine, it's very difficult to be a raw eater. But the foods are amazingly tasty and stunning to look at.

I've found that cashews, an indispensable item for making raw desserts, give me the creaminess I miss from dairy. Raw nut butters are available now in shops, but home-made is always fresher. Below are several ways you can put this fabulous butter to use. Please use caution – it's highly addictive!

MAKES APPROX 250 G/8 OZ/1 CUP

225 g/8 oz/2 cups cashew nuts, untreated, unroasted

4 tablespoons flax (linseed) or hemp oil or coconut juice (the water inside a coconut), or fresh orange juice (enough to make a paste),

2 tablespoons honey or agave nectar

dash of sea salt

Blend the cashew nuts in a coffee grinder or food processor until the mixture is like fine beach sand. Keep the machine running and add a drizzle of oil or juice, enough to create a paste. Add the sea salt and honey or agave nectar and store in a tightly lidded jar in the refrigerator.

Variations

You can also use the following nuts or seeds for nut butters as long as they have not been roasted, oiled or smoked: almonds, peanuts, walnuts, macadamia nuts, sesame seeds, pumpkin seeds, sunflower seeds, hulled hemp seeds. Buy the freshest nuts and seeds, put them in a tight container or plastic bag, and store them in the freezer until you need them.

Nutty Variations

NUT ANGLAISE

250 g/8 oz/1 cup of cashew nut butter

125 ml/4 fl oz/½ cup of coconut juice (water from inside a coconut) or rice milk

Thin out the cashew nut butter, with the coconut juice or rice milk. Mix well until smooth.

You can use this for topping fruits or tarts. By reducing the liquid to 40 ml/3 fl oz/⅓ cup, you can also spread this on the bottom of your fruit tarts.

CASHEW NUT GLAZE

300 ml/10 fl oz/1⅓ cups coconut juice (water from inside a coconut) or fresh fruit juice

a tip of a sharp knife's worth of turmeric or powdered saffron

seeds from ½ vanilla pod

100 g/4 oz dates, pitted and chopped

3½ tablespoons cashew nut butter

2½ tablespoons fresh lemon or lime juice

zest of ½ lemon, finely chopped

In a blender or food processor, blend the juice with the turmeric or saffron. Don't add too much turmeric or it will make the glaze bitter – it's only used here for colour. Scrape out the seeds from the vanilla pod by running your knife along its length, add them to the blender and whiz again. Add the rest of the ingredients and whizz until smooth, adding a bit more liquid if you find the glaze is too stiff.

NUT WHIPPED CREAM

175 g/6 oz/1½ cups cashew nuts, untreated, unroasted

125 ml/4 fl oz/½ cup coconut juice (water from inside a coconut) or orange juice

175 ml/6 fl oz/⅓ cup agave nectar

Place the cashew nuts in a bowl and cover with the filtered water. Let them soak for at least 4 hours. Drain, and blend in a food processor with the coconut juice or orange juice and agave nectar. Whip until pale and fluffy. Serve over ice cream, tarts or with fruit salads.

Luscious Lemon Cream

This recipe is so melt-in-your-mouth, I was tempted to call it lemon melt. The lemon zest, juice and margarine (or coconut butter or ghee) blend so beautifully together, you'd swear it had butter in it. I layer it in ice cream sundaes topped with crushed meringues, fold it into Mock Whipped Cream (page 148), or simply spread it on a piece of bread or a Proper Scone (page 58).

MAKES 750 G/1½ LB/3 CUPS

2 organic eggs

50 ml/2 fl oz/ cup lemon juice

zest of 1 lemon

115 g/4 oz/½ cup unrefined golden (superfine) caster sugar

70 g/2½ oz/⅓ cup margarine or ghee or coconut butter

Put the eggs in a bowl. Place the lemon juice, zest and sugar in a heavy pan, bring to the boil, and slowly pour over the eggs, whisking constantly. Return the mixture to the pan and put back on a medium heat. Whisk constantly until thickened, anywhere from 5–8 minutes – the custard will resemble a crème patissière and will leave a trail or ribbon as you lift your whisk. Strain through a fine-meshed sieve and leave to cool for about 15 minutes.

Pour the lemon mixture into a food mixer fitted with a whisk attachment. Turn the machine on high and add the margarine in 4 or 5 additions. Let the machine run for another 2 minutes or so until the mixture is creamy smooth. You can freeze it for about 1 month.

Homemade Adzuki Beans

Adzuki beans are small and burgundy-coloured. They're used in Japanese cuisine, especially for auspicious occasions such as New Year. They're ground into a flour to be used in baking cakes, or cooked whole and puréed into a paste. In the macrobiotic diet they are the most 'yang' of all the beans. It is also said that they convert carbohydrates into energy and have a very high level of calcium and potassium. The adzuki bean helps the body get rid of excess water and relieves kidney problems.

Adzuki beans are used in a lot of Japanese sweets. Since there is very little land for grazing in Japan, and eating meat was highly discouraged by the Buddhist tradition, dairy foods were traditionally never eaten. Also homes never had ovens, therefore desserts were never baked! Rice and adzuki beans were vital in the making of Japanese sweets. These two combined offer the body all the essential amino acids it needs. Adzuki beans almost always have a touch of sugar added to them, even when they are eaten alongside a savoury dish. As a sweet they are most often puréed with sugar to make the traditional paste called anko. They can be made into a red jam and layered between pancakes (dorayaki) or puréed and mixed with agar agar and cut into cubes (yokan). It is also used in mochis, a yummy, gooey, Turkish delight type confection made from sweet rice flour and sometimes rolled in sesame seeds. The slightly bitter Japanese green tea is drunk with desserts made with this paste, to cut its sweetness.

Place 85 g/3 oz/½ cup of adzuki beans in a bowl and cover with lots of water. Leave to soak overnight. Drain the water off, place the beans in a pot and cover with 450 ml/16 fl oz/2 cups of fresh water. Bring to a fast boil, then lower the heat and allow to simmer for about 45–60 minutes or until soft. The Japanese cook these beans with a piece of kombu (seaweed) to make the beans more tender, but soaking them is good enough.

To make the sweet paste, drain the water and add 115 g/4 oz/½ cup of unrefined golden caster (superfine) sugar and a pinch of sea salt to the beans. Stir the beans for about 15–20 minutes or mash them over medium heat until you get a chunky paste, about 20 minutes.

Variations

Churn the sweet paste along with your ice cream base, or top a scoop of Wild Orchid Ice Cream (page 120) with a dollop of this lovely red bean paste.

Vanilla Buttercream

The technique used in making this buttercream is what makes it taste like the real thing. Don't be put off by the different steps – if you have a food mixer and everything is set up before you start, you'll be fine – and you'll be rewarded with the silkiest buttercream, which also freezes for up to a month. See below for a variety of flavours.

MAKES 4 CUPS

115 ml/4 oz/½ cup filtered water

400 g/14 oz/1¾ cups unrefined golden caster (superfine) sugar

1 vanilla pod, split in half lengthwise

7 organic egg yolks, at room temperature

225 g/8 oz/1 cup margarine, coconut butter or ghee, softened and cold

Put the water, sugar and vanilla pod into a small pan and bring to the boil. Stir at first to dissolve the sugar, then leave it to boil. Meanwhile, place the egg yolks in a food mixer fitted with a whisk attachment. Check your syrup – if it has reached 120°C/245°F or nearly hard-ball stage, take the pan off the heat. Turn your mixer to medium speed for a few seconds, just to blend the eggs. Remove the vanilla pod, then carefully pour the hot liquid down the side of the mixing bowl while the machine is still running. Once all the syrup has been incorporated, increase the speed to high and beat for about 15–20 minutes until the mixture cools to room temperature. You can check this by simply touching the base outside of the bowl. It's that easy. Scrape the inside of the vanilla pod with the back of a knife and blend the seeds into the mixture.

The margarine, coconut butter or ghee needs to be cold yet soft. You can get this consistency by stirring or almost 'kneading' it with a spatula on a clean kitchen worktop or marble board. Turn the machine back on, this time on low, and add the margarine to the mixture in 5 or 6 batches. Increase the speed to medium and let it cream for a further 10 minutes. You now have a beautiful creamy smooth buttercream, but it will be on the soft side. Chill it in the refrigerator for about 30 minutes before using.

This buttercream freezes up to 1 month. To serve from frozen, thaw, and whip for a few minutes before using.

Variations

Coffee Buttercream: Prepare the Vanilla Buttercream as above and add ¾ teaspoon coffee extract or 2 teaspoons instant coffee granules dissolved in 1 tablespoon hot water.

Maple-spiced Nuts

I love nuts. They're great as nibbles served with drinks and yummy as a topping for ice creams and cakes. These have the sweetness of maple sugar and the headiness of allspice that makes you think you're in Vermont on a beautiful autumn afternoon. Put these nuts in pretty little packages and offer them to your loved ones – they're so easy to make and you'll get so many compliments that you may even be tempted to start your very own business! Why not?… Maple Nuts Inc!

MAKES APPROX 400 G/13 OZ/4 CUPS

1 organic egg white

1 teaspoon vanilla extract

115 g/4 oz/²/₃ cup maple sugar, or light brown sugar

pinch of sea salt

zest of 1 small orange

½ teaspoon ground allspice or ¼ teaspoon each of ground cloves, ground cinnamon, ground ginger and ground nutmeg

pinch of cayenne pepper

450 g/1 lb/4 cups nuts – macadamias, pecans, hazelnuts or peanuts

Preheat the oven to 170°C/325°F/gas mark 3. In a large bowl, mix together the egg white, vanilla extract, maple sugar, salt, orange zest and spices. Add the nuts and mix thoroughly until they're well coated. Place the mixture on a non-stick baking tray or a silicon baking liner, spreading it around evenly. Bake in the preheated oven for about 30 minutes, tossing the nuts around from time to time to make sure they brown evenly. Remove from the oven and leave to cool. When quite cold (the nuts will get drier), break up and store in an airtight container.

Variations

If you are allergic to eggs, replace the egg white with 1½ tablespoons of light olive oil or sunflower oil or coconut butter. These nuts may be stored for up to 10 days in an airtight container.

Homemade 'Nutella'

I was about five when I came face to face with my first jar of Nutella. I'll never forget the way it smelled as I spread it on a piece of baguette. I just could not believe how divine it tasted. Later, I realized I could forgo the bread and just eat it off the spoon either at room temperature or hard, chilled, from the refrigerator. Until I was grown up enough to read the label and see that it contained partially-hydrogenated oil as well as artificial flavours. All other chocolate spreads contained soy, even natural organic ones. I found out that, in fact, Nutella is a commercial form of the famous Gianduja chocolate. It was created during the Napoleonic wars, when the British army blockade created a shortage of cocoa all over Europe. In Turin, in Italy, in the region of Piedmont, where they are famous for their hazelnuts, they fixed that problem by creating a cheap substitute for chocolate. They ground hazelnuts to a fine paste and mixed them with cocoa to create a delicious heady chocolate that is now considered a true delicacy.

MAKES APPROX 3 CUPS

115 g/4 oz/½ cup coconut butter

45 g/1½ oz/⅓ cup cocoa powder

85 ml/3 fl oz/½ cup honey

115 g/4 oz/½ cup semi-sweet chocolate, chopped, e.g. Valrhona's Gianduja or Manjari 64% minimum cocoa solids

3 tablespoons hazelnut oil

pinch of sea salt

2 teaspoons vanilla extract

175 g/6 oz/¾ cup hazelnut butter, either store-bought, or made by putting 225 g/8 oz/2 cups skinned and roasted hazelnuts into a food processor and whizzing to a paste

Heat the coconut butter with the cocoa powder and honey, then stir in the chopped chocolate. Add the oil, salt, vanilla extract and hazelnut butter, and stir until smooth. Don't allow the mixture to boil, as the base will burn – you just need to warm the mixture gently enough to melt the chocolate.

Pour into a jar and store in the refrigerator. Bring to room temperature before spreading.

Spread on crêpes, use to top ice creams and basically do everything else you did with Nutella!

Simple Syrup

Although extremely simple, as the name suggests, this syrup can be your saviour. It can be used in sorbets, for poaching fruits, for thinning coulis, and for soaking layered cakes such as Le Fraisier (page 64). Once prepared, it can be stored in the refrigerator for months, or it can simply be made as you need it. This recipe is for plain syrup, but I'm also giving you some variations to try which will bring out the best in any ordinary cake, even a dried-out one!

MAKES 500 ML/17 FL OZ

> 225 g/8 oz/1 cup unrefined golden caster (superfine) sugar
>
> 225 ml/8 fl oz/1 cup water

Combine the sugar and water and stir to dissolve the sugar. Bring to the boil and as soon as the mixture reaches boiling point, turn off the heat and allow it to cool. If you want to use the syrup immediately and don't have time to let it cool, use just half the water, turn off the heat and add the other half in the form of ice cubes. Stir until dissolved.

Here are some interesting flavours you may want to try adding to the syrup before boiling:

- 1 stalk of lemongrass, split in half, plus 1 teaspoon lime zest
- ½ vanilla pod, slit lengthwise
- zest of 1 small lemon
- 2 tablespoons kirsch, Cointreau or rum
- 1 tablespoon cocoa powder or instant coffee granules
- 1 cinnamon stick

Golden Agave Caramel

Mexicans have been cultivating the agave for centuries and consider the plant to be sacred and its liquid a purifier of the body and soul. The Spanish took its juice and fermented it into tequila. The wonderful thing about the agave is that it is fructose in its purest form, about 90%. The fructose that we know is mostly refined from corn. Agave is safe for diabetics as it has an incredibly low GI (glycaemic index) level and a mild sweet clean taste that goes with everything.

The trick with an agave-based dessert is to eat it on an empty stomach, as it takes on the value of any high-glycaemic food you may have consumed immediately before. So try not to eat fructose straight after a large meal. Eat agave-based sweets between meals or with other low-glycaemic foods to get the maximum effect. Drizzle agave nectar on anything you like. You can also substitute it for regular sugar in such things as lemonades and teas and other hot drinks.

The caramel below is light golden and is made in minutes. The basic recipe can be drastically changed by using other liquids instead of the milk, such as fresh fruit juices – orange, strained passion fruit, pineapple, even pomegranate!

MAKES 250 G/8 OZ/1 CUP

> 325 ml/11 fl oz/1⅓ cups agave nectar
>
> 60 ml/2 fl oz/¼ cups rice or almond milk,
> or coconut juice
>
> 1 tablespoon expeller-pressed coconut oil,
> (not virgin), or ghee

Place the agave nectar in a saucepan and bring it to the boil. It will become foamy and bubbly. Keep stirring it with a wooden spoon until it starts to deepen in colour. As with all caramels, it's best to be attentive because it can suddenly become too dark. Once it has deepened to an amber colour, take it off the heat and pour in the rice milk or coconut juice and the coconut oil or ghee. The mixture will steam up, and as soon as the bubbles have subsided, place it back on the heat and stir for a few seconds. Pour it into a heatproof jar and use it as soon as it cools, or store it in the refrigerator and bring it to room temperature again before using. You can also serve it hot by quickly heating it on the stove or in the microwave.

Vegan Royal Icing Sugar

I always get a little nervous when I have to use raw eggs in my recipes. This one is completely safe, as it's eggless, but still gets the job done beautifully. Mix it with some food colouring and create different hues. You'll be amazed at the new natural food colourings, which are just as bright and fun as the artificial ones. And why should one eat brillaint blue no.4 and allure red no.2 food colours when you can have a rainbow of different colours made from nature itself – ruby red from beets, yellow from turmeric, bright green from spinach. There are sugar crystals that are also natural, and silver balls made from real silver. Go ahead and have fun with your friends or your kids knowing that what you enjoy eating is also good for you!

MAKES APPROX 2½ CUPS

450 g/1 lb/4 cups unrefined icing (confectioners') sugar

60 g/2 fl oz/¼ cup agave nectar or

light rice syrup

2½ tablespoons water

food colouring

Whisk the icing sugar with the agave nectar and the water until you get a thick paste. Add a little more water if necessary.

This icing may be used in place of any ordinary icing such as in cakes on piped on to cookies. Cover any remaining icing with clingfilm so that it doesn't dry out until you are ready to use it. It will also keep for several days in the fridge.

Frosting in a Flash

This is the quickest buttercream or frosting you can ever make. Use expeller-pressed, naturally refined coconut butter for a neutral taste. Coconut oil is made up of short-to-medium-chain fatty acids, (which are digested easily) that our bodies use for energy, and it does not raise cholesterol levels.

MAKES ABOUT 2 CUPS

60 g/2 oz/½ cup cocoa powder

dash of sea salt (optional)

325 g/11 oz/2⅔ cups golden icing (confectioners') sugar

115 g/4 oz/½ cup expeller-pressed coconut oil, at room temperature

85 ml/3 fl oz/⅓ cup rice, almond or coconut milk

2 teaspoons vanilla extract

Sift the cocoa powder, salt (if using) and sugar. Beat the coconut butter with an electric whisk and gradually add the cocoa mixture, milk and vanilla extract, mixing until smooth, about 1–2 minutes. Refrigerate for a while if it's too soft. If it's still too limp, add up an extra 2 tablespoons of cocoa powder.

For regular vanilla frosting, follow the recipe above, omitting the cocoa powder. Add 2 teaspoons of vanilla extract or scrape out a knife tip's worth of vanilla seeds. Blend in the juice and finely chopped zest of ½ lemon and only add a little milk to get a smooth consistency.

Quick Fruit Spreads

Who makes jam nowadays? Although it's such a lovely and loving thing to make, it just takes too much time. This recipe will give you an intense fruit spread that is super-quick to make and keeps very well in the refrigerator. You can use it for spreading on toasts and muffins. Add agave nectar, maple syrup, rice syrup or sugar to taste. Some fruit spreads don't need sugar at all. It really depends on the type of fruits you choose or have around. Try to use unsweetened unsulphured dried fruits. The colours may not be as bright, but they're so much tastier and better for you. If you have any fresh fruit handy, drop them into the food processor along with the dried fruits for an even fresher taste. Just remember that it won't keep as long. Store all jams in the refrigerator or freezer.

TUTTI FRUITY

85 g/3 oz/½ cup dried apricots

85 g/3 oz/½ cup dried plums or prunes

150 g/5 oz/1 cup dried berries (cherries, blueberries, strawberries)

Place the fruits in a bowl and cover with filtered water. Leave to soak for at least 6 hours or overnight. Drain off the water and purée the fruit in a blender or food processor until smooth, together with sweetener to taste. Blend a little less if you like your spread chunky.

TROPICAL SPREAD

175 g/6 oz/1 cup dried pineapple

85 g/3 oz/½ cup dried mangoes

45 g/1½ oz/½ cup desiccated coconut

350 ml/12 fl oz/1½ cups coconut juice or pineapple juice

Place the fruits in a bowl and cover with the coconut juice or pineapple juice. Leave to soak overnight. Place the fruits and the juice in a blender or food processor and purée.

EARTHY SWEETNESS

300 g/10 oz/2 cups dried dates, pitted and chopped

150 g/5 oz/1 cup raw (untoasted) sesame seeds

Place the dates and sesame seeds in a bowl and cover with filtered water. Soak for about 4 hours and not more than 6. Strain off the liquid, reserving some of it, and purée the date and sesame seed mixture. Add a bit of the reserved liquid if the texture is too thick. Orange juice makes a nice substitute for water.

Bébé Meringues

The best thing to do when making meringues is to use 'old' eggs. Don't be alarmed, this is just a French expression meaning whites that have been separated from their yolks and left in the refrigerator for a couple of days. They make a much fluffier meringue. Don't expect snow-white ones, as you are using unrefined golden sugar, but to get them as pale as possible, bake them overnight on the lowest setting.

Serve them on their own or with Sundaes (page 136). You can also pipe them to make baskets and fill them up with chestnut purée or crush them into Eton Mess with Crème Patissèrie and strawberries.

MAKES 30–35 MINI MERINGUES

> **4 large organic egg whites, at room temperature**
>
> **225 g/8 oz/1 cup unrefined golden caster (superfine) sugar**
>
> **½ teaspoon vanilla extract**

Preheat the oven to 130°/250°F/gas mark ½. Prepare a baking tray lined with baking parchment or a silicon baking liner. Attach a small star nozzle to a piping bag and set aside.

Using a KitchenAid (or other food mixer) with a whisk attachment, or a hand-held electric whisk, whip up the egg whites until they form soft folds. Keep the machine running and slowly add the sugar in stages, ending with the vanilla extract, whisking until the eggs form stiff glossy peaks. With a large rubber spatula, spoon the meringue into the piping bag and pipe mini-rosettes about 5 cm/2 inches in diameter onto the prepared baking tray. Leave about 2 cm/¾ inch space between the meringues.

Bake in the preheated oven for about 1½–2 hours or until very pale gold, rotating the tray a few times to ensure the meringues bake evenly.

7

potions

Heavenly potions are drunk all over the world, for so many reasons. Sometimes we forget how good they are for us and how much **fun** we can have trying out new ones. From Chocolat Chaud to Green Goddess, Tapioca Ball Shakes and heady Glühwein, the potions in this chapter are packed with tons of **vitamins** and **minerals**. Sip these liquids slowly or gulp them through a fat straw… but remember that potions are the greatest **cleansers**, **energizers** and regenerators of our system. Whether to warm you up or cool you down, to **detox** your system, or simply to quench your thirst, these potions are **absolutely delicious!** Serve them in beautiful clear glasses to show off their **brilliant** colour. Make a big pitcher to share with friends and loved ones, for all to **enjoy**.

Tapioca Ball Shakes

Bubble tea, boba milk tea and pearl milk are some of the other names for this drink. Originating in Taiwan in the '80s, it quickly spread to Japan and other parts of Asia like wildfire. Bubble bars have sprouted like mushrooms all over the US and Canada and will hit European shores very soon.

The pearl, or ball, refers to the tapioca or cassava root found at the bottom of the glass. The pearls have been caramelized to a dark blackish colour and have a consistency between jelly babies and jelly – they are sucked up through a thick straw and give you something to chew on between sips. These drinks are usually made with either black or green tea and are shaken in a martini shaker with crushed ice cubes.

There are endless variations, and here are just a few to get you started. You can experiment to see which flavour combinations you like best. There are just four easy ingredients in making these shakes: **Liquid sweeteners**, such as honey, sugar syrup, agave nectar or rice syrup. **Liquids**, such as strong brewed Chinese black tea, green tea, Rooibos or coffee. **Flavours**, such as fruits and fruit juices, almond meal, chocolate powder or extracts and **ice**, crushed or whole.

BASIC BUBBLE TEA RECIPE

225 ml/8 fl oz/1 cup black tea, green tea or espresso

7–8 ice cubes, crushed

225 ml/8 fl oz/1 cup rice or almond milk

sugar, to taste

60 g/3 oz/½ cup tapioca pearls

Pour everything into a martini shaker and shake for a few seconds. Pour into a large glass. Use this as a base and add anything you want to it such as non-dairy cream, ground almonds or fruit juice.

You can make a Chocolate Almond variation by omitting the tapioca pearls and adding 2 tablespoons cocoa powder and 2 tablespoons of ground almonds

HONEYDEW

60 g/3 oz/½ cup tapioca pearls

1½ tablespoons unrefined golden caster (superfine) sugar dissolved in 175 ml/6 fl oz/ ¾ cups green tea

150 g/5 oz/1 cup chopped honeydew melon

1 thin slice fresh ginger

5 ice cubes

Place the tapioca pearls in a tall glass. Whisk the rest of the ingredients in a blender until smooth and pour into the glass. You can substitute the melon with chopped mangoes, pineapples, green apples, mixed berries or even fresh orange juice.

COCONUT

350 ml/12 fl oz/1½ cups black or green tea

7–8 ice cubes, crushed

115 ml/4 fl oz/½ cup coconut milk

2 tablespoons coconut powder

60 g/3 oz/½ cup tapioca pearls

2½ tablespoons agave nectar or honey

Mix everything in a martini shaker and serve. You can add any kind of berry purée for a creamy fruity taste and bright colour.

Decaffeinated Coffee

On any given day, as much as 80% of the world's population is walking around caffeinated by one means or another. Many are turning to decaffeinated coffee to try and kick the caffeine habit, or consume less of it. I have escaped becoming addicted to coffee and consider myself very blessed. If I drink it, my heart beats so quickly it feels as though it will pop out of my chest. I do like the taste, however, and on occasion I order a decaffeinated coffee instead. But there are so many reports on how unhealthy this is for the body.

There are four ways to decaffeinate coffee. The two most common methods use methylene chloride and ethyl acetate. Although these methods retain most of the coffee flavour, they are also known to give you cancer. Companies who use these methods do not need to tell you which method they've used on the label, and some would even label their coffee as 'naturally decaffeinated', since ethyl acetate is made from fruit – but if you touch it, it will burn your fingers. The two other methods used in the industry today are the Swiss water method and the supercritical CO_2 method. These leave no toxic residue and can remove as much as 99.9% of the caffeine. The latter is easiest on the environment, as it uses less water, and these two methods are the only ones that can be certified organic.

Remember that there is no legal definition for decaffeinated coffee. It can have anything from 96 to 99.9% of the caffeine removed. That's 2–4 mg per cup. Regular coffee has 65–120 mg of caffeine per cup. When in doubt, choose organic decaffeinated coffee. Organic coffee tastes better, is better for the rainforest and is one of the ways to restore the earth's eco-structure. Shade coffee, as the name suggests, is coffee grown under the canopy of trees, which protects the area's biodiversity and helps prevent erosion of the soil. Sun coffee production destroys the forest by cutting down the trees in order to maximize the growth of coffee berries, as well as eroding the soil, polluting the rivers with chemicals from fertilizers and removing the natural habitat for birds and other animals. If you're not drinking organic Fair Trade shade coffee, you are consuming sun coffee. A simple switch can make a world of difference.

Decaffeinated coffee can can be substituted for regular coffee in desserts, syrups, ice creams, cakes, even buttercream. I find non-dairy milks too light to whiten my coffee or tea, so below is a concentrated dairy-free condensed milk that does the job. Use it in coffees, cappuccinos, hot or iced green tea and rooibos.

Sweetened Condensed Milk

Method 1

Boil 685 ml/24 fl oz/3 cups of rice or almond milk in a pan with 115 g/4 oz/½ cup of unrefined golden caster (superfine) sugar, stirring frequently until reduced by two-thirds. Take it off the heat, add 1 teaspoon of vanilla extract and stir until smooth.

Method 2

Mix 225 ml/8 fl oz/1 cup of Vance's DariFree milk powder with 115 ml/4 fl oz/½ cup of boiled filtered water. Mix 115 g/4 oz/½ cup of unrefined golden caster (superfine) sugar with 1 teaspoon of vanilla extract. Mix the milk and sugar mixtures together and stir to a smooth consistency.

Whichever method you use, keep your condensed milk in an airtight jar in the refrigerator.

Japanese Green Tea

Green tea has been consumed in the East for 5,000 years and is now the second most popular beverage in the world. It is known to have many health benefits, such as lowering cholesterol, boosting the immune system, helping prevent cavities and tooth decay, as well as fighting against certain forms of cancers. It is 200 times more potent than vitamin E in fighting free radicals; it protects the liver against damage, contains lots of antioxidants which neutralize free radicals, and is also a natural fat-burner. Green tea is being used more and more in foods – it has a distinct taste that goes very well in sweets and desserts.

There are four main types of green tea in Japan: Matcha, Gyokuro, Sencha and Bancha. Some come as tea leaves, others in powder form or tea bags. You'll need to experiment to find out which ones suit your tastebuds. You can also get green tea leaves that have been naturally decaffeinated using the water method, which locks all the benefits and taste in. I like to drink green tea instead of coffee because it contains half the amount of caffeine and doesn't give me the shock and jitters of regular coffee. Its smooth taste is clean and refreshing on its own, but you can also drink it with non-dairy creamer (or any dairy-free substance). Green tea sodas and soft drinks are very popular in Japan, and it is also used to flavour cakes and ice creams – even chocolates.

The best way to enjoy green tea is to use a Japanese teapot called a kyusu. Put the tea leaves in the pot, pour hot water over them, put the lid on and wait a couple of minutes before pouring out into tea cups. An ordinary teapot is also fine. If you want to get to the very best flavour from green tea, you will need to adapt the temperature of the water according to the type of tea you are drinking.

SENCHA
Use water that has been boiled to 71°C/160°F and let the tea brew for only a minute before drinking.

GYOKURO
Use water at 43°C/110°F and brew for about 2–3 minutes.

MACHA GREEN TEA POWDER
Put 1 teaspoon into a teacup and add a cup of 71°C/160°F water to it. Stir with a bamboo spoon, not a metal one as it may alter the taste of the tea.

BANCHA TEA
As it is a low-grade tea, it just needs boiling water and a few seconds of steeping in the pot.

Masala Chai

The first time I came across this tea was in India. It's so popular there that they have street vendors by the name of chaiwallahs who sell it in earthen cups at nearly every street corner. The word chai comes from the Chinese word cha, meaning tea. Masala, in India, is the name for any spicy blend. In fact the word garam masala comes from the Persian word garm (meaning warm) and masaleh, a mix. The Persian mix is a combination of such things as saffron, rosepetals, cinnamon and other delicate spices. It was brought over to India by the Moghuls but became a stronger spice blend.

This tea is heavily spiced but absolutely delicious and soothing. Every Indian family has its own version of masala chai, so there is no wrong way of making it. Try to choose a robust tea such as Assam that can handle the mixture of strong spices and marries well with dark sugars. If you're avoiding caffeine, try a naturally decaffeinated house-blend or rooibos instead.

SERVES 4

2.5 cm/1 inch chunk fresh or dried ginger

1–2 whole black peppercorns

1 cinnamon stick

3 cloves

2 cardamom pods

680 ml/1¼ pts/3 cups filtered water

2 tablespoons black tea, rooibos or decaffeinated house blend tea

115 ml/4 fl oz/½ cup rice milk or almond milk

Muscovado, turbinado, rice syrup, dark agave nectar or sorghum molasses to taste

In a pestle and mortar, crush the ginger, peppercorns, cinnamon, cloves and cardamom. Put the water into a saucepan and add all your crushed spices and the tea. Bring to the boil for about 1 minute and turn the heat off. Cover and let all the flavours infuse and come together, about 2 minutes. Add the milk and sugar, bring the liquid back up to the boil, strain and serve.

Thai Iced Coffee

MAKES 4 SERVINGS

enough water and ground coffee beans to make strong fresh coffee for 4 people

4 cardamom pods

Take the cardamom seeds out of the pods, place them in your coffee maker along with the coffee, and let it brew. Leave to cool, then pour into a tall glass over ice and lighten with condensed milk to taste.

Pomegranate Love Potion

It's said that Aphrodite, the Greek goddess of love, planted the seeds of the pomegranate on the island of Cyprus. Historically the fruit is mentioned in many cultures and religions. The pomegranate tree is said to have flourished in the Garden of Eden, and Greek and Persian mythology refers to the pomegranate as representing life and marriage. In Judaism, its seeds are said to number 613, representing each of the Torah's 613 commandments. It is also a symbol of life and fertility in Christianity and of blessings in Buddhism. The pomegranate has been used as a dye, medicine, food and even as insignia. Originating in Persia and central Asia, it migrated outwards towards India, northern Africa, China, Europe and the Americas, where they grow excellent varieties in California. It is still an intricate part of Middle Eastern cuisine and life. In fact, pomegranate juice bars are as popular in Iran as Starbucks is in the US.

The pomegranate is packed with vitamins. An excellent blood-purifier, it contains more antioxidants than red wine, green tea, noni juice and cranberry juice, and is full of vitamin C! Drink pomegranate juice straight up on the rocks or as the smoothie below.

SERVES 4

150 g/5 oz/1 cup small frozen pineapple chunks

680 ml/1¼ pints/3 cups unsweetened pomegranate juice, preferably fresh (see below)

175 ml/6 fl oz/¾ cup fresh orange or tangerine juice

3–4 strawberries or a handful of raspberries

½ teaspoon agave nectar or sugar, to taste

Place all the ingredients in a blender and whizz.

Variations

There are many brands of pure unsweetened pomegranate juice available in Middle Eastern stores, but you may want to juice your own. The plumper and heavier the fruit, the juicier and sweeter it is. Make sure the skin is taut and has no visible marks on it. The easiest and best way to juice a pomegranate is the same way you would juice a grapefruit or orange. First put on an apron, then cut the fruit in half and use an electric or manual citrus juicer. I like the old-fashioned ones, with a handle you pull down in order to squeeze the juice out.

Another method is to gently roll the pomegranate on a hard surface such as a table. Keep rolling it around this way and that, so that you crush the seeds inside and release the juices. You'll end up with a limp soft fruit filled with liquid. Make a very small hole in the widest part, keeping the crown or top end the right way up, and suck the juice out, solo!

Rooibos

Also known as redbush tea, rooibos grows on vibrantly green bushes in the region around Cape Town in South Africa. The Khoi tribe were known to be the first to use rooibos, but their secret vanished along with them. In 1772 a botanist by the name of Carl Humberg rediscovered it and brought it back as a beverage, but it wasn't until nearly 200 years later, in 1968, that a South African mother, Annique Theron, realized that rooibos had the power to calm her crying and insomniac baby and went on to publish her findings in a book called *Allergies – an Amazing Story*. Since then doctors have discovered that rooibos is full of antioxidants and flavonoids, similar to those in green tea, which has made it highly sought after. It is known to soothe the body's reaction to allergies such as eczema – in fact it sometimes goes by the name of herbal allergy tea. It relieves stomach cramps, has amazing anti-ageing properties, and is even used as a spice, meat tenderizer and marinade. Unlike other teas, rooibos has limited tannin, is naturally caffeine-free and is rich in alpha-hydroxy acid, which we all know is excellent for the skin.

Rooibos comes in plain and also in a variety of different flavours from chocolate to caramel, orange, masala and lemon chiffon. You can replace rooibos in anything that calls for tea such as iced tea, sauces and even Tapioca Ball Shakes page 168. Try it in your fruit punch or cocktails.

SERVES 4

Boil 4 cups of filtered water with 1–2 teaspoons rooibos tea. Cover and let steep for about 4–5 minutes. Rooibos has the tendency to become bitter if brewed for too long.

Raw Almond Smoothie

This creamy smoothie can be made with rice milk or almond milk. You can add cocoa powder or even carob powder to the mixture make a rich chocolate drink instead. Lace this smoothie with orange-blossom water to make an authentic Moroccan speciality, or with almond extract for a fuller taste. Try using rapadura sugar or agave nectar to see what real sugar really tastes like before it is separated from some of its nutrients. You can use this recipe as a base for numerous other smoothies – strawberry, coffee, rooibos, chocolate, ginger, flaxseed, even chai. Experiment and come up with your own favourite version.

SERVES 2

30 g/1 oz/¼ cup raw almonds or cashews

175 ml/6 fl oz/¾ cup almond or rice milk

⅓ teaspoon vanilla extract, almond extract or orange-blossom water

pinch of ground cinnamon

1 teaspoon sugar, rapadura or date sugar, or ½ teaspoon agave nectar, or to taste

5 ice cubes

Mix all the ingredients in a blender until smooth. Serve immediately.

Green Goddess

Raw juice therapy, which has been steadily gaining in popularity, involves replacing some meals exclusively with a raw unprocessed fruit or vegetable juice. This way all the vitamins and enzymes are kept intact. It's also a fabulous way to get leafy greens into your diet in one go or a way to fool your kids into eating more vegetables. Kids love the murky green colour. Tell them it's swamp water and they'll drink it right up.

SERVES 2

3 celery stalks

1 banana

½ large cucumber

handful of fresh spinach
or 115 g/4 oz/½ cup frozen spinach

1 bunch parsley or coriander (cilantro)

1 tablespoon spirulina

225 ml/8 fl oz/1 cup filtered water

Chop the celery, banana and cucumber and place in a blender. Add the spinach, parsley or coriander and spirulina and blend until smooth. If the mixture is too thick or getting stuck, simply add a little water or vegetable juice, push everything down with a spoon and blend again until smooth.

Chocolat Chaud

The original hot chocolate recipe was a mixture of ground cocoa beans, water, spices and peppers. The word chocolate is derived from the Mayan word xocoatl, and the word cocoa comes from the Aztec word cacahuatl. Thus the word chocolate comes from choco (foam) and atl (water). The Olmecs, the oldest civilization in the Americas, were the first to use cocoa. Later, the Mayans used it in their drinks and also as a form of currency. We all know kids who do that now! Cocoa was drunk on very special occasions or ceremonies.

The Mexican emperor Montezuma introduced Cortes to chocolatl in a giant gold goblet. Cortes later wrote to the King of Spain: 'The divine drink builds up resistance and fights fatigue. A cup of this precious drink permits a man to walk for a whole day without food.' He filled his ships with cocoa beans and headed home to Spain, where the Spaniards sweetened chocolate with sugar and warmed it up. Even now we have special occasions when we drink hot chocolate – when we meet up with a foodie friend or want to snuggle up indoors when it's cold outside. I would say that a cup of this heavenly drink permits a woman to shop the high streets without any food!

SERVES 2–4

> **550 ml/1 pt/2½ cups rice milk or almond milk**
>
> **60 g/2 oz/¼ cup golden caster (superfine) sugar**
>
> **115 g/4 oz/½ cup dark (bittersweet) chocolate e.g. Valrhona 61% minimum cocoa solids, finely chopped**
>
> **2 tablespoons cocoa powder**

In a saucepan, boil the rice or almond milk with the sugar until hot. Add the chocolate and the cocoa powder and heat until the mixture starts bubbling. Take it off the heat and with a hand-held blender, whiz the hot chocolate for about 2–3 minutes until frothy. Top it off with some Crème Chantilly (page 148). Serve right away, while it's hot.

Fruit Smoothie Base

Fruit smoothies are not what they used to be. They don't need to be filled with tons of sugar and dairy products to be enjoyed. They're now mixed with all sorts of nutritious ingredients that make them complete meals on their own. Hemp or rice powders add lots of protein to your shakes – gone are the days when you had to rely on soya protein alone. Add extra vitamin C or ground flax seed to your smoothies. A shot of spirulina does wonders for the body, as does good old vitamin C powder.

SERVES 2

1 large banana

150 g/5 oz/1 cup fruits (mangoes, berries, pineapple, honeydew melon)

225 ml/8 fl oz/1 cup coconut juice or filtered water or any nut milk

2 tablespoons agave nectar, or to taste

2 tablespoons lemon or lime juice (omit if using nut milk)

1 shot plain protein powder, rice or hemp

Chop the banana and place in the freezer with the rest of the fruits for at least 3 hours.

Thaw the fruits for 5–10 minutes before blending with the rest of the ingredients. Add more liquid if you'd like your smoothie on the runny side.

Liquid Detox

This is for the days where you've overdone it and want to feel cleansed and revived: a diuretic vitamin-C-packed mixture of lemon juice, aloe vera, mint and cucumber, all sweetened with a touch of low-glycaemic agave nectar. The cucumber is an excellent blood cleanser and draws excess water out of your system. Aloe vera, used by the Egyptians for treating burns and infections, is another fabulous remedy, as it also helps the digestive system and normalizes stomach acidity. Refreshing mint clears the skin and is both calming and stimulating to the function of nerves, stomach and liver. You'll feel as though you're drinking something from a top-notch spa.

SERVES 2–4

7–10 mint leaves

450 ml/16 fl oz/2 cups filtered or mineral water

85 ml/3 fl oz/⅓ cup aloe vera juice

1 teaspoon agave nectar, or to taste (optional)

10 cm/4 inches cucumber, finely shredded

juice of 2 lemons

Crush the mint leaves in a pestle and mortar or cut them into very small shreds. Mix with the mineral water, aloe vera juice, agave nectar, shredded cucumber and lemon juice and drink up!

Glühwein

This Austrian mulled wine goes by the name of vin chaud in France. It goes down amazingly well after a day on the ski slopes, while you rest by the log fire. I suggest you don't use a very expensive wine, since you'll be infusing it with all sorts of spices. The traditional recipe calls for rum as well as brandy, but that might make you tipsy far too quickly to be able to enjoy it to the full. Besides the fact that red wine is delicious, its antioxidant properties are good for you too. Drinking red wine in moderation can reduce the risk of heart attacks and even protect against the common cold.

SERVES 4–6

8 cloves

1 orange, cut into 8 slices

1 bottle of organic red wine such as Cabernet Sauvignon or Merlot

115–150 g/4–5 oz/$\frac{1}{2}$–$\frac{2}{3}$ cup unrefined golden caster (superfine) sugar or light brown sugar

2 star anise

2 cinnamon sticks

dash of nutmeg

Push the cloves into the skin of the orange slices. Put them into a pot with all the other ingredients except the nutmeg, and simmer on a very low heat until the mixture is very hot – but don't let it boil, or the alcohol will evaporate.

Turn the heat off, place the lid on the pan, and let the spices infuse the wine for about 30 minutes.

Grate in a little nutmeg, gently bring the wine back to simmering point, and serve hot.

top sites & addresses

The following information will help you track down ingredients and gadgets and find the answers to your questions about gluten-free, dairy-free and soya-free lifestyles.

US

Organizations Helpful guidelines, pamphlets and annual vendor information with listings of gluten-free products and recipes.

- Celiac Disease Foundation (CDF), 13251 Ventura Blvd, suite #1, Studio City, CA., USA 91604. Tel: (818) 990-2354, www.celiac.org

- Gluten Intolerance Group of North America (GIG), 15110 – 10th Avenue, SW, suite A, Seattle, WA., USA 98166 Tel: (206) 246-6652, www.gluten.net

- www.FoodAllergy.org (list of hidden ingredients that can cause allergies and intolerances).

Online Stores

- www. Authenticfoods.com carry flours such as Garfava flour, as well as baking supplies and cookery books.

- Both websites www.arrowheadmills.com and www.bobsredmill.com stock all the flours you need, as well as catalysts and gluten-free flour mix. Bob's carries excellent dried fruits, nuts, and spices.

- ✳ www.ener-g.com carries kosher certified products. A wide variety of cereals, mixes, baked goods such as cookies, bagels, pizza crusts, and milk powders.

- ✳ www.missroben.com or www.allergygrocer.com has an amazing selection of gluten-free flour mixes from Bette Hagman and others. Buy your natural food colours from Dancing Deer Company and decorative sugar crystals from India Tree. You can also find buckwheat and poha flakes, whipped marshmallow cream made from rice syrup, Vance's DariFree and white chocolate chips by Oppenheimer.

- www.nspiredfoods.com has Tropical Source vegan chocolate, gluten-free dairy-free baking chips, Sunspire candies, nut and seed butters.

- www.Vancesfoods.com carries Vance's DariFree.

Shops and Markets

Whole Foods has many of the ingredients you will need. Others such as Wild Oats and Trader Joe's also carry great items such as organic chocolate, gluten-free flours and dried fruit and nuts.

Gadgets

www.Jbprince.com has an impressive selection of gadgets for the professional chef. They carry anything and everything you need for your kitchen and you don't have to be in the business to be able to buy from them. www.surlatable.com has everything from ingredients to pans, moulds and flan rings as well as Silpats and the latest trends in kitchen utensils.

UK

Organizations Helpful information, leaflets and listings of gluten- and dairy-free products, sources and recipes.

- www.Coeliac.co.uk (great links to international organizations around the globe). PO Box 220, High Wycombe, Bucks HP11 2HY, Tel: 0870 444 8804

- www.dairyfreeuk.com (a forum including articles and links about about dairy-free information.)

Online Stores

- www.barbaraskitchen.com and www.dietaryneedsdirect.co.uk have joined forces and offer almost all of the ingredients you need! All the flours in my recipes are sold here, from tapioca to potato starch flour. Buckwheat and poha flakes, hulled hemp seeds and oil, flax (linseed) oil, hazelnut oil, raw almond butter, agave nectar, palm fat, coconut milk, milk powder, rapadura sugar, unrefined caster (superfine) sugar (golden and brown), agar agar, chestnut purée, gluten-free breadcrumbs, Vance's DariFree milk powder, various dried fruits, xanthan gum, Manuka honey, gluten-free ice cream cones, carob powder, natural food colouring, palm fat, FOS (Fructo Oligo Saccharide) and more!

- www.clearspring.co.uk sells agar agar, kuzu, green tea, amazake, lovely fruit purées and lots of other Japanese products that are organic and GM free.

- Dancing Deer Company natural food colouring, Oppenheimer white chocolate and India Tree sugar crystals can be ordered through www.missroben.com in the US.

- www.dovefarms.com Gluten-free flour mix.

- www.goodnessdirect.co.uk. Kosher, egg-free products, adzuki beans, dairy-free milk alternatives, rice syrup, coconut milk and butter, quinoa flakes, Biona margarine, Ener-G egg replacer, xanthan gum and more.

- www.green&blacks.com and www.Valrhona.com are the best for chocolate.

- www.alotofchocolate.com has alternative sections on soya-free, gluten-free and dairy-free chocolates, Fair Trade and kosher.

- www.rejuvenative.com has a variety of addictive organic raw butters such as pure hemp, cashew, tahini, sunflower, pumpkin and home-made mixtures. Contact Graham Weinberg at www.red23.co.uk for nutritional advice and natural products in the UK.

- www.veganstore.co.uk. Sells soya-free Vegan Supreme marshmallows and Tropical Source chocolate are sold on this site.

Shops and Markets

- Fresh & Wild UK is now owned by Whole Foods USA (www.wholefoodsmarket.com/stores/freshandwild) and has many shops around London.

- www.Planetorganic.com has many of the ingredients you need, such as sugars, coconut juice (Dr Martin's Coco drink), coconut milk and cream, gluten-free flour, rice and agave nectar and more.

- Larger stores such as Waitrose, Safeways, Tesco and Sainsbury's carry Doves Farm gluten-free flour, Billington's unrefined golden caster (superfine) sugar, oils, spices, coconut milk, coconut cream and ghee.

- Chinese, Japanese and other Asian markets are worth a trip. They stock many flours, such as tapioca and sweet rice flour (mochiko). You will find agar agar and kuzu, lemongrass and other fresh herbs and spices. Caramelized tapioca pearls, coconut milk, cream and juice, green tea, konnyaku (devil's tongue) and rice paper wrappers are also easily found.

- Indian markets carry big containers of ghee, chickpea flour and good spices.

- Middle Eastern markets offer amazing fresh spices such as saffron and cinnamon at a fraction of the price. Also find salep powder, pomegranate juice, tahini paste, rosewater and orange-blossom water.

- African markets carry tapioca (cassava flour), coconut juice and other hard-to-trace flours.

Gadgets

- www.divertimenti.co.uk have everything from muffin tins, cake tins and trays as well as some silicon moulds. They carry silicon liners! They have great ice cream machines and KitchenAids, and a very knowledgeable team to help you with all your needs.

- www.lakelandlimited.com has a large selection of general baking supplies.

- www.ifyoucare.com has wonderful chrome-free aluminium and parchment liners and paper cases made from recycled paper.

hidden ingredients to look out for

There are many hidden ingredients you'll want to avoid in order not to have any adverse reactions. Some may seem obvious, others are a bit trickier. Learn to read labels like a pro and you'll always know what you are eating.

The following is a list of items or terms that may contain gluten, dairy/casein or soya, unless otherwise stated. Remember, some brands may be OK and others may not, for example, chocolate chips or icing (confectioners') sugar. Always check the labels before purchasing:

- **anything with the word 'wheat', except buckwheat**
- **Artificial colours or flavours**
- **Barley**
- **Bean Curd**
- **Bulgur**
- **Baking powder with gluten**
- **Bicarbonate of (baking) soda with gluten**
- **Calcium caseinate**
- **Canola oil (rapeseed oil)** *Oh shit!*
- **Chocolate chips with milk solids**
- **Chocolate syrup with milk solids**
- **Couscous**
- **Dextrins, maltodextrin and modified or edible food starch***
- **Edemame**
- **Food colourings**
- **Graham flour**
- **Icing (confectioners') sugar**
- **Kamut**
- **Malt and malt extract and flavouring**
- **Marshmallows**
- **Miso** *???*
- **MSG**
- **Natto**

- **'Natural' flavours**
- **Oats**
- **Okara**
- **Rice puff cereals (certain brands)**
- **Rice syrup made with barley**
- **Rye**
- **Spelt**
- **Store-bought sauces**
- **Soy-based whipped toppings**
- **Soy sauce**
- **Spices and seasonings**
- **Tamari**
- **Tempeh**
- **Textured vegetable protein**
- **Tofu**
- **Triticale (a hybrid wheat with rye)**
- **Vegetable oil (usually contains soy bean oil)**
- **Vanilla extracts (some contain alcohol made from gluten)**
- **Vitamins**

Look for gluten free vanilla extract

*Certain starches need to be sourced as they can also be made with corn, tapioca and potato instead of wheat.

index

acknowledgments

First of all, I'd like to thank all those who have bought *Sweet Alternative*. I hope this book is useful to you and most importantly that you have fun cooking these recipes.

I'd like to thank my agent Louise Greenberg for making me redo my proposal 100 times until I finally got it right. I will never forget your patience and support.

Many thanks to Lorraine Dickey for believing in this book and to her fantastic team at Conran Octopus who helped me pull this together: Katey Day, Jonathan Christie, Sybella Marlow and Chloe Brown. Thank you also to Lucy Gowans for your grace and professionalism and Lisa Linder for capturing those little details and making my dishes look delicious. My cousin Taher who dressed up for the 'photo shoot' and still stayed around even though he had to wash the dishes.

I'd also like to thank the following people for making this book happen:
My parents for their love and support: my wonderful mom whose eclectic cooking revealed so many different cultures to our family; and Rod who unfailingly supported me in anything I wanted to do. I am forever indebted to you both.

My uncle Mike Bargani for encouraging and allowing me to follow my dream of becoming a chef. No amount of words could express my gratitude. My late father for being a true food lover and passing it on to my brother and me. Thank you to my lovely brother for his generous hospitality during my stay in California.

Jean and Roland Hughes who helped me as if I was their own daughter. Jean, without you there could have been no Sweet Alternative. Thank you for all the recipe testing, conversions and help with the photo shoot. Roland, for all your fabulous photos.

My 'foodie' friends Rana, Anjum, Leyla and Maryam who never ever got tired of talking food with me and brainstorming over new ideas. Behzad Mohit for his hospitality and welcoming me into his lovely home in Marin County. I have been blessed to have such good friends and family who have been by my side and were willing guinea pigs to taste my 'experiments'.

Thank you to the all the chefs I have worked with and who have inspired me with their passion, notably Laurent Duchenne, Francois Gaertner and Bruno Dreyer.

Jim Keeble, Alessandra Galloni and Roxanna Shahpour for letting me know that you were there if I ever needed you.

Everyone in the alternative food industry who, with their dedication, vision and beliefs, have changed the way we eat today. Thank you Dr Martien Witsenburg for your eye opening speech on 'margarines'.

Last but definitely not least, a great big thank you to my wonderful husband Paul for absolutely everything. From putting up with my late night 'ideas' and months of travel, to eating sweets even when you didn't feel like it. Thank you for praising me to boost my confidence and also for always giving me your honest opinion. This book would have never been written without your love and support.